We have little to say when we begin life's runway, and little to say when we end our runway, but we do have control on the runway. Michelle Ray's new book, *Lead Yourself First! Breakthrough Strategies to Live the Life You Want* is bang on the money. Buy it, read it, and learn from it.

—DR. PETER LEGGE, OBC, CPAE, CSP,
HoF Speaker/Author/Businessman

Michelle Ray offers realistic ways to overcome common workplace challenges. Her life-changing parables are a must-read for growing your career in today's economy.

—JEFF MOWATT, bestselling author of *Influence with Ease*

If you are ready to master your own destiny and turn self doubt into self mastery; Michelle's magic way of telling real-life stories with life lessons should immediately jolt you out of any situation where you feel stuck. Don't miss this read if you are ready to make a change.

—ELAINE ALLISON, CSP, bestselling author of *The Velvet Hammer,
PowHERful Leadership Lessons for Women Who Don't Golf*

Michelle Ray is an *authority* on inspiring one to truly get the life they want. Clear, inspiring, and easy to read. This is the kind of book that takes a hold of your insides so that you do not give up on yourself. You will find you'll keep this book over your many years. Why? Because it works.

—VALERIE CADE, CSP, workplace bullying expert and
author of *Bully Free at Work*

Pragmatic, down-to-earth, simple, and effective techniques. Everyone can get great ideas; quick and easy to use. If you want to make dramatic changes in your life this book provides you with the essential tools.

—RON COLEMAN, author of *Building Your Legacy: Lessons of Success
from the Contracting Community*

Michelle Ray speaks to you at a gut level. She gets right to the point and finds your blind spots. You will love how she writes and be inspired by how she motivates. I hope you enjoy reading *Lead Yourself First* as much as I have.

—LINDA EDGECOMBE, CSP, HoF, author of *Shift or Get Off the Pot!*
Simple Truths About Getting a Life

A call to arms for anyone pursuing a life of freedom. Take Michelle's advice. Get out! You weren't born to live in a box. You need to break free!

—WARREN MACDONALD, adventurer, speaker, and
bestselling author of *A Test of Will*

Lead yourself straight to this book! Michelle Ray has created a leadership book with a difference. It is filled with inspirational stories, humor, and thought-provoking lessons. She tells us tales of ordinary folk who are reminder that each of us can be extraordinary. Read it and be inspired to make change!

—PAMELA CHATRY, Executive Managing Director, *eWomen Network*
Vancouver Metro and Coquitlam

Michelle helps us pull ourselves up out of mediocrity and demand more for our lives. A great message!

—JANE ATKINSON, author of *The Wealthy Speaker*
and *The Wealthy Speaker 2.0*

We all have "moments of truth in our lives" and those moments of truth have the power to change our lives forever. In those moments of truth we choose, consciously or unconsciously, to be a victim, survivor, or a thriver. If you want to be a thriver, this book is a must-read.

—DR. BRAD MCRAE, CSP, Director, *The Atlantic Leadership*
Development Institute

Michelle Ray's *Lead Yourself First* shares thought-provoking stories and practical advice that make you want to jump out of your rut and into a rich, expansive life worth living! And I say, why merely survive when you can truly *thrive*—financially, professionally, and emotionally? It sure energized me.

—MICHELLE CEDERBERG, speaker, coach, and author of *Energy Now!*
Small Steps to an Energetic Life

In my work as a professional speaker, I meet many colleagues who talk a good game but Michelle Ray has been on the real "field." *Lead Yourself First* is an honest, no-hype guide to real life that may be a bitter pill to swallow as you reflect on your current reality, but like good medicine, worth the effort. If you want to change your "view," read this book!

—ALVIN LAW, motivational speaker and author of *Alvin's Laws of Life*

Michelle Ray's book, *Lead Yourself First* is a great read. It reminds me of the push I sometimes need to step outside of my comfort zone and follow the path I want, not just the path I think I should be traveling. Many of her stories give me that "aha" moment and her humorous take on the good and the bad make me smile as I'm reading.

—STEPHEN HAMMOND, speaker, consultant, and bestselling author
of *Managing Human Rights at Work: 101 Practical Tips
to Prevent Human Rights Disasters*

If you're looking for inspiration and practical strategies to stay positive during these challenging times, *Lead Yourself First! Breakthrough Strategies to Live the Life You Want* is the book for you. In this accessible, and easy-to-read book, Michelle shares relatable personal stories to illustrate the power of personal leadership. She shows readers how to develop a "can-do" mindset to accelerate personal and professional success.

—ERICA PINSKY, author of *Road to Respect: Path to Profit (How to Become
an Employer of Choice by Building a Respectful Workplace Culture)*

Thomas Paine wisely told us that "Character is much easier kept than recovered." Author Michelle Ray reminds us . . . "Character first, Title second." Personal leadership is a highly personal choice. Michelle Ray leads us to expand our possibilities in all things by making that choice every moment of each day.

—KARYN RUTH WHITE, motivational comedian, author, entrepreneur

Michelle has written the perfect book for these uncertain times. For anyone who is tired of being at the mercy of their environment and is ready to take charge of their success and their life this is a must-read. Michelle's expertise and experience shines through as she shares how to break free and become the leader of your own life.

—LYNN ROBINSON, Founder, The Robinson Group Training
and Consulting Corp. Co-Founder, Life Without Regrets

Powerful doses of practicality, seasoned with dollops of humor and touches of whimsy, Michelle Ray draws upon her years of first-hand experience to provide a realistic and no-nonsense primer on how to break free of the mental and emotional handcuffs that stop you from accomplishing what you truly want to achieve. Use her simply laid-out strategies to switch on, step up, and stand out.

—MERGE GUPTA-SUNDERJI, MBA, CGA, CSP leadership and workplace
communication expert and author of *Why Does the Lobster
Cast Off Its Shell?*

Lead Yourself First!

Indispensable Lessons
in Business and in Life

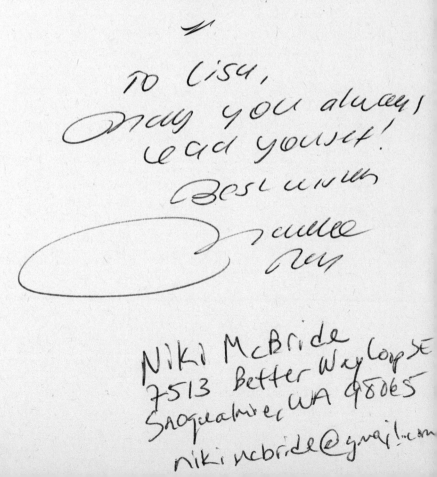

To Lisa,
may you always
lead yourself!
Best wishes

Niki McBride
7513 Better Way Loop SE
Snoqualmie WA 98065

niki.mcbride@gmail.com

Lead Yourself First!

Indispensable Lessons
in Business and in Life

Michelle Ray

CHANGE
MAKERS
BOOKS

Winchester, UK
Washington, USA

First published by Changemakers Books, 2014
Changemakers Books is an imprint of John Hunt Publishing Ltd., Laurel House, Station Approach,
Airesford, Hants, SO24 9JH, UK
office1@jhpbooks.net
www.johnhuntpublishing.com
www.changemakers-books.com

For distributor details and how to order please visit the 'Ordering' section on our website.

Text copyright: Michelle Ray 2014
www.leadyourself1st.com

ISBN: 978 1 78279 703 6

A CIP catalogue record for this book is available from the British Library.

Managing Editor: Gordon Thomas
Editing: Patti Frazee
Proofreading: Nora Ayanian-Shawn
Design: Fiona Raven

Printed and bound by CPI Group (UK) Ltd, Croydon, CR0 4YY

We operate a distinctive and ethical publishing philosophy in all
areas of our business, from our global network of authors to
production and worldwide distribution.

Contents

This book is dedicated
to the memory of my parents,
Bela and Helena Ray.

You are in my thoughts each and every day
as I recall your extraordinary life journeys.
You exemplified the meaning of leading oneself first.
Your resilience through unthinkable hardships
and eternal optimism prevail. I know you would have been
so proud to read and hold this book.
Your spirit and love will live forever in my heart
and are evident on every page.
I miss you both beyond words.

Foreword

Over the span of my career I have met individuals from all walks of life who strive to make a difference. Some experienced privileged upbringings with the proverbial "silver spoon" at hand; others survived unimaginable challenges. Regardless of their circumstances, I have noticed that there are certain people who embrace an innate ability to create opportunities that profoundly impact their world and that of those around them.

Michelle Ray is one such individual. She immediately stood out from the crowd as I heard her speak at my eWomenNetwork Success Summit event in Vancouver, Canada. Her message on self-leadership struck a deep cord in me as she reminded the audience that it *is* possible to control their reality when they recognize the power of perspective. Michelle captivated her listeners by allowing them to tap into their imagination. She truly walked her talk by delivering to the audience of entrepreneurs a powerful message of inspiration, education, and above all, the courage to believe in themselves.

As the founder and CEO of eWomenNetwork Inc., my personal journey has taken me to the brink; spiritually, emotionally, and financially. I faced the challenges and risks of starting a business as a solopreneur early on, and today lead one of the largest multimillion-dollar networking organizations for women business owners in the world. There is no question that resilience is an asset when it comes to taking risks, both personally and professionally. However, I have learned that by acquiring the courage to live my life authentically, I attract exactly what I need in order to rise above uncertainty, disappointment, and despair.

In *Lead Yourself First!*, Michelle shares her inspiring life stories—experiences that revealed the importance of making values-based decisions. They offer a refreshing level of "human-ness" in business, blended with rich, "how-to" content that gives the reader permission to explore their own life-journey to help discover their unique purpose and passion in life.

Michelle's wisdom, humor, and common sense is now available to anyone who is ready to say "yes!" to opportunity and is willing to rise from setbacks to see—perhaps for the very first time—the vast horizon of their own potential. Without a doubt, this book will provide you information, strategies, and techniques that will equip you with a deeper understanding of yourself in relation to success, money, family history, and your higher purpose.

The joys of living *your* life and leading yourself first are only pages away!

Sandra Yancey
Founder & CEO, eWomenNetwork Inc.
eWomenNetwork.com

Acknowledgments

I am extremely grateful to many people who encouraged me for years to write a book. I knew, however, that "writing for the sake of writing" never felt comfortable to me. I wanted to write on a subject I was passionate about, rather than conforming to the notion that every speaker needs to have a book. My views on leadership ultimately compelled me to tell my story from a personal standpoint, with a goal to help people learn specific strategies to become the leaders of their own lives. This is distinctly different from books regarding leading others, or being a better leader in the workplace.

Leadership goes deeper than a job title. Leadership is a state of mind that requires discipline, self-acceptance and above all, the willingness to create change. When we are standing on the fence, knowing there is something bigger that we want to accomplish, I have discovered that all we need is the right push to get us going. It certainly was the case for me.

My deepest thanks first and foremost goes to Patti Pokorchak, my professional colleague who provided the nudge I needed via a LinkedIn message to attend a book boot camp in Toronto facilitated by book coach Les Kletke. During that transformational weekend I also met Janet Rouss, Carol Ring and later Jennifer Spear, all members of our self-appointed Skype book group. Thank you to my amazing group: Patti, Janet, Carol and Jennifer who were on-line every week for six months, reviewing my writing and making insightful recommendations for many chapters in this book. I could not have completed this journey in cyberspace without each one of you.

My profoundest appreciation for the rich insights, wisdom and unwavering support provided by Gordon Thomas, my editor, advisor and book project manager extraordinaire, as well as Patti Frazee, whose editorial skills and uncanny ability to help me unravel stories and content worked brilliantly to produce the final outcome. Thank you as well to Fiona Raven, book designer, for her professionalism, patience and ability to articulate my vision into the brilliant cover design. You all worked hard to roll out the red carpet for me and now readers everywhere will have the opportunity to appreciate my book.

I wish to express my gratitude to Sam Horn for her wisdom and guidance. Thank you, Sam, for helping me clarify the essence of my message and allowing it to shine through in my writing and anecdotes.

I am also thankful for my brother, Mark and my sister-in-law Regina, who provided assistance with the narrative and stories regarding Mom and Dad. We laughed and cried as we reflected on their indescribable legacy. To my nieces, nephew and grandchildren, you each inspired me with your gorgeous imagination and unconditional love to stay the course. Thank you for reminding me to be true to myself.

Last but by no means least, my greatest thanks to my significant other, Brian Libin, for your love, tolerance, encouragement and understanding. I couldn't have persevered without your thoughtfulness and forbearance during the many long days and nights, including my five-day writing stint at the Holiday Inn in Surrey, BC. You are truly one of a kind and I am blessed to have you as my husband.

Introduction

In Memory of Stan

In November 2003, I was on my way home from a five-day business trip, passing through three time changes as I flew west to Vancouver. It was 5:00 p.m. on a Friday afternoon. I was tired and certainly in no mood to practice personal leadership. I was at Regina Airport, joining the other passengers heading zombielike into the metal detector. As we begrudgingly obeyed the robotic commands to remove electronic equipment from carry-on bags, I noticed the people ahead of me laughing uncontrollably. The hysterics clearly weren't normal. The closer I got to the front of the line, the louder the giggles became. That's when I noticed Stan the Security Man. I watched as he single-handedly entertained every passenger as each one engaged in the well-rehearsed ritual of removing shoes and bags for scanning, followed by a personal screening that we would either pass or fail.

As I walked through the metal detector, the alarms sounded, the lights flashed . . . chaos broke loose. Stan was waiting for me to walk through, bemused by the fact that I had no idea why I had set the machine off. I was panicked, but he simply looked at me and smiled. Then, he placed his hands to his chest and cupped his "breasts" without saying a word. I looked at him, wondering what he could possibly be doing. Would I be strip-searched? Was some deep humiliation coming my way? Then it hit me. Underwire bra!! I didn't know I had the power!

I immediately convulsed with laughter and my impatience and exhaustion vanished. I asked Stan if the machines were different in Regina, as my undergarments had not previously registered at any other Canadian airports.

We engaged in a lighthearted conversation as Stan examined the contents of my bags. I happened to be carrying a pink magic wand (doesn't everybody?). Stan removed the wand and proceeded to ask: "Are you the fairy godmother?" More laughter. When I explained my line of work as a professional speaker, Stan became very excited and asked if I was like Anthony Robbins, to which I replied: "not exactly." He requested my business card and said he would look me up.

By this point I had to hurry for my flight and thanked him for our conversation. As I began running for the gate, Stan called out: "You have a beautiful smile!" Without turning around, I yelled, "thank you!" Now bound for Vancouver, I did not expect to see or hear from Stan again.

I arrived home three to four hours later, walked into my office and turned on my computer. As my email began downloading from the entire week, I noticed the following message, at the very top of the list:

-----*Original Message*-----
From: Stan Lindley
Sent: Friday, November 7, 2003 10:52 PM
To: Michelle Ray
Subject: You

Michelle, I am the Security Guard who went through some of your "stuff" at the Regina Airport this evening. I really enjoyed your website. Very good! Inspiration is a desired item these days. I used to be in the RCMP and ended up in

Re/Max selling in Edmonton. I loved motivational tapes and listened to them all the time. Life was good then all hell broke loose, my son took his life, my marriage ended, and I lost my job as a Provincial Govt. Fraud Investigator. I am rebuilding my life but it is slow and laborious. I was on disability for almost 3 years, and had to take a Security Job to keep going. I am trying desperately to move on, but feel overwhelmed by my age some days. I came back to Saskatchewan because this is where I grew up and my mother is still here although in failing health.

She is 85 and has Alzheimer's. I am now her caregiver, and life is hard.

You were a momentary bright light this evening, and just wanted you to know that I would give anything to know that I could climb up that ladder just one more time, and get the most out of life. Maybe I could catch one of your seminars should you ever come back to this area again.

Thank you for the smile, it was worth a fortune to me. I will keep going. . . . I just wanted you to know you made a difference this evening.

Yours truly,
Stan Lindley

A great deal of correspondence ensued between Stan and me. I asked Stan's permission to tell his story and he generously agreed. Stan Lindley was the leader of himself. He exemplified the principles of "me" management in every facet of his life as he unselfishly went about his day-to-day responsibilities. During the course of his work in Regina and subsequently Edmonton airport, Stan continued to have an impact on complete strangers until he was stricken with a rare form of cancer that took him at age 61.

He wrote to let me know that when he was told he had only three to four months to live, he knew he would be unable to continue working, although it was his wish to "continue to make a difference." Stan personified the meaning of "leader" as he harnessed the ability to take charge of his thoughts, and consequently his actions, in any situation. Character first. Title second. This was Stan the Security Man.

How often do we take stock and consider the impact of one person on the totality of how we choose to be in the world? Unfortunately, all too often when we have special encounters like this, we fail to see or appreciate the example. Therein lies the premise of this book: Lead yourself first, because no one else will.

1

Why Should We Sip from a Teacup When We Can Drink from a River?

—C.D. BALES (STEVE MARTIN IN THE MOVIE *ROXANNE*)

Dream Big, Don't Settle

In 1987, after living a year in the United States, I was completely enamored and planned to continue to live and work in New York City. But my romantic dreams of living in the U.S. were shattered when I was unable to secure a work permit or permanent residency. I had to return to Australia and suddenly felt like the rejected lover. Leaving the U.S. was a devastating blow. I felt depressed and lost, even as I tried to settle back into my old life in Australia.

One gloomy, rainy Sunday afternoon in Sydney I treated myself to a matinee. As a Steve Martin fan, I looked forward to his latest movie, *Roxanne*. Based on Edmond Rostand's book *Cyrano de Bergerac*, Martin played the role of Charlie aka C.D. Bales (taking his initials from Bergerac). Charlie was the fire chief of a small town. He was blessed with a zany sense of humor, sharp wit, a gift for writing, and an impossibly long nose. Charlie's life was missing one major element: romance.

I found myself identifying with Charlie's character. He was physically awkward and self-conscious, yet he had an irrepressible spirit. His deep desire for a relationship with his friend Roxanne resonated with my newfound dream of living in North America; a dream that sometimes seemed so unattainable it had become a love affair just out of reach. As I watched the movie, I immediately became captivated by the clever dialogue and magnificent scenery. I was so moved by the beautiful setting that I literally heard myself sighing throughout the film. I was completely entranced by the backdrop of the quaint houses and storefronts nestled amongst mountains and surrounded by magnificent evergreen trees.

I could hardly wait to find out where the movie was filmed. As the credits began to roll and the theatre emptied, I was transfixed, waiting with heightened anticipation. *Where* is *this place?* I just had to know.

By now the cleaning crew was working behind me, sweeping up the empty boxes of popcorn. I was still in my seat and I could hardly stand it. Finally, the very last lines appeared on the screen: "Filmed entirely on location in Nelson, British Columbia, Canada." At that moment I vowed that one day I would go to this place.

Initially, I didn't realize how much the film would impact my life. Even though I had returned to my former life and my former job in Australia, I felt a profound sense of emptiness and disappointment. A part of me knew I had to accept the fact that a life in New York wasn't meant to be. I was cautious about trying to return to the United States, not wanting to feel that disappointment again. Yet, I was constantly pulled to return to North America.

While my family desperately hoped I would get the travel bug out of my system, the desire to try again was too strong. One day my co-worker Lucy told me about the Canadian working holiday program available to anyone in Australia between the ages of eighteen and twenty-nine-and-a-half. I was surprised to learn that such a program existed. Canada had not been on my radar, but after seeing *Roxanne*, I became excited and decided to look into the program. I wasn't fazed by the fact that I knew absolutely no one in Canada.

As soon as I received confirmation that my one-year visa had been approved, I began making plans. I placed an advertisement in the classified section of the local Vancouver newspaper, seeking a sublet arrangement for the summer. I only received two replies, but one was from a young man who was traveling to Australia and wanted to rent out his apartment. Within a few days, Joe and I had a sublet agreement in place.

On July 7, 1990, I arrived in Vancouver. It happened to be the same day Joe was leaving for Sydney. His entire family, the Grad clan, was waiting for me at the airport. When I entered the arrivals hall, Joe's folks were holding a giant poster that read "Welcome to Canada, Michelle." I was overwhelmed by their generosity and warmth. After saying our goodbyes to Joe, my newly adopted relatives took me shopping for groceries at the local supermarket. We then went to Joe's place and they made sure I was comfortably settled. The weather was magnificent and it felt like summer would never end.

The following morning I walked down to English Bay and around Stanley Park for the better part of six hours, mesmerized by the seawall. Evergreen trees were everywhere. I smiled and thought of Nelson, British Columbia; I knew that it was time for me to visit the place where my dreams had been rekindled.

With a very long drive ahead of me, there was one hurdle

I hadn't considered: driving on the opposite side of the road. This was so daunting to me that I absolutely did not want to drive in the city for fear that I would end up staring head-on into oncoming traffic. So, I boarded a bus bound for the Okanagan Valley, my first stop on the way to the Kootenays and Nelson. I stopped in Kelowna to visit some friends and get a good night's sleep. The next day I went to the rental car office to pick up my vehicle.

I began my journey surrounded by the spellbinding landscape of mountains and evergreens; I was so excited to be heading in the direction of Nelson. As I climbed further into the mountains, my excitement was met with white-knuckle driving through narrow, winding mountain roads. Then there was the unpredictable weather; it was often raining and sometimes I had to navigate, on the opposite side of the road, through thick fog.

Anticipating a five-hour journey, I arrived in Nelson at night-fall—some ten hours later! But the next morning when I looked out the window of the Nelson Youth Hostel, I was overcome by emotion. I was looking at the very same scenery I had seen in *Roxanne*. I did the *Roxanne* walking tour and visited the Fire Hall. There were photographs of the local fire department staff with Steve Martin and the cast. Just like C.D. Bates, my dream had come true. My romance with my new country had truly begun.

I cast my mind back to the movie theatre in Sydney where I had first seen Nelson. As I stood outside the Fire Hall chatting with the staff and volunteers on duty, I grasped the serendipity of the moment. For the first time, I reflected on the sequence of events that had led me to this beautiful place.

When I went to the movies that afternoon, three years earlier, I was still recovering from the disappointment of not being able to stay in New York. As Canada revealed herself through the big screen in the form on Nelson, my spirit came alive. Not long afterwards, Lucy told me about being able to work in Canada. Prior to *Roxanne,* I thought I had a vision of where I wanted to be; I just didn't realize the plan that was unfolding was even better than anything I had conceived on my own.

Sometimes we think we have life all figured out, and when things don't go our way it's easy to give up and wallow. Have you ever embarked on a journey, thinking you had planned your destination meticulously, only to find that you hit a few unexpected bumps along the way? Have you been resolute about achieving success somewhere, only to give up because things didn't work out the way you intended? Have you stayed the course or allowed yourself to be sidetracked?

Keeping Your Sights on Your Vision

During my years working at a radio station in Sydney, I had the privilege of forming relationships that have endured to this day. I met wonderful clients who wished me every success when I left Australia. I recall having lunch with one client shortly before my departure and, as we discussed my pending adventure, she revealed something about herself that I never knew, even though we had been doing business together for years.

Julie worked in an advertising agency for more than twenty years. Her office had breathtaking views of Sydney Harbour and she didn't have to battle traffic as her workplace was walking distance from her home. She was an excellent buyer on behalf of her own clients and could do her job blindfolded. Julie disclosed her secret desire: to live in England and pursue her passion for photography. When I asked her what was stopping her, she informed me that it was "too late." I sensed this was a painful subject, so I did not press her.

Although Julie was thrilled for me, I could see the sadness

in her eyes. In her mind, she decided that her ship had passed and there was no point thinking about what might have been. Whenever I reflect on this conversation, it reminds me of the fact that Julie had the opportunity to follow her aspirations, yet she chose a different path. Her justification for not making her vision a reality was the passage of time.

It is possible to transform your regrets into a new reality. It becomes a question of deciding what you want your reality to look like.

Realigning Your Vision to Go with the Flow

When you have it in your mind that plans must unfold in perfect order and those plans are quashed by events that are outside your control, feeling disappointment is human. Making an effort to fully appreciate this turn of events may at first seem impossible. Valuing an experience that manifests as a setback may feel ludicrous. However, when you recognize that *emotions* are dictating your interpretation of an unexpected outcome, it becomes easier to put the obstacle into perspective.

When I received word from my attorney in New York that my application for a work visa had been rejected, I took the news personally. I began talking myself out of my dream and gave myself an even harder time for trying to make it happen. I returned to Australia with my tail between my legs, heading on a downward spiral that seemed to have no end.

At one point I felt as though I was on the precipice of depression because I could not shake the enormity of the loss. I could only interpret the situation from the negative. The air had been sucked out of my balloon and there was a period when I viewed the entire New York experiment as nothing short of a monumental failure. No one could talk me out of my state of defeat. The only thing that kept me going was hope.

My working holiday in Canada was not the turning point nor the consolation prize; it was the catalyst for a fresh perspective on what had actually transpired. I have learned that it is not possible to look at situations objectively when I am in a highly emotional state. I could not glean any

driving to Nelson on the right side of the road, I was definitely outside of my comfort zone. However, I wasn't about to turn around after coming that far! As night fell, there were fewer cars on the road and it took every ounce of my energy to stay focused on the right side. In the end, it was the trip of a lifetime and the culmination of my dream.

As you pursue your vision and encounter difficulties along the way, remember there is a big difference between these two questions: "Why is this happening?" versus "Why is this happening *to me*?" The hurdles that present themselves are of consequence; they do not necessitate giving up. In the words of C.D. Bales: "Why should we sip from a teacup when we can drink from a river?" Whatever your Nelson may look like, be sure to take in the view.

Who Turned Out the Lights?

Dedicated Slaves

Soon after graduating from University, I was between advertising jobs and working part-time at the front desk of In-Shape Gym. I had moved back in with my parents because I could no longer afford to pay rent. I definitely needed to search for new employment. One day I saw an ad in the job classisfieds: *State Sales Manager for Australia's Fastest Growing Advertising Company.* My fingers couldn't get to the typewriter fast enough! The recession had taken a toll on the advertising industry and jobs like this were a rare find. I knew it would be a highly sought-after position and thought I should give it a shot.

I was working at the gym when the call came; I was asked if I was available for an interview the next day. I contained my excitement and remained calm while I checked my (empty) calendar to confirm a 2:00 p.m. appointment the next day. As soon as I hung up the phone, I began jumping up and down.

I called my parents and all my friends to tell them the great news. The idea of being a *manager* was so appealing to me.

As I walked down Pitt Street for the interview, I already visualized my beautiful large office, brand-new company car, and high-paying salary. I arrived outside the building and checked the address. I looked back up at the building and back down at the address; I was hoping there was a mistake. The four-story building that stood before me was grey and drab; frosted, barred windows, some cracked, had thick, abandoned cobwebs draped around the edges. This building looked as though it was about to be condemned.

The paint was peeling off the walls in the lobby and several of the fluorescent lights flickered as I made my way to the elevator. When the doors opened to the second floor, the hallway was almost pitch-black. The light fixture was broken and a lonely bulb swayed from the hanging wires. To my left, I saw glass doors and headed in that direction, unsure of whether I was on the right floor. The sales department receptionist greeted me with a half-hearted half smile. "Hi luvvy. You here for the manager job? Take a seat. You're next." Her words said one thing, but this was a less-than-warm reception.

I sat down and almost went through the chair—the cushion was completely worn and hard as a rock. I took in the surroundings and noticed the carpets were ripped in several places. The windows were filthy and several were cracked. I could see huge piles of dust balls and dirt on the windowsills.

Although it was a large space, the office was devoid of activity with the exception of a young man in one corner office, talking on the phone. At the opposite end was another office. The door was closed. The remaining space was an open-plan area comprised of ten partitioned cubicles, each furnished with a desk, chair, and telephone. The cubicles were largely empty; this place was a ghost town. Within a few minutes, the receptionist's phone rang. "The big boss is ready to see you now."

She escorted me down the hall where the boss, Conrad, appeared in the doorway and smiled broadly. He extended his hand and enthusiastically shook mine. The dilapidated surroundings I had noticed earlier became invisible; suddenly, all I could see was Conrad's confident demeanor and 1,000-wattage smile. The interview lasted for over an hour and went brilliantly. We negotiated my package, which included a brand-new car—just as I had imagined! I was ecstatic. I started my job as the new State Sales Manager one week later.

Sound perfect? Well, a few glitches began to appear. First of all, the knives came out on Day One. I discovered that the previous manager I replaced had been demoted to make room for me. Apparently, it was impossible to fire her, even though she had run the department into the red and turnover was rampant under her leadership. She decided to stay on in a sales representative role and it was my job to keep her motivated. Any attempt on my part to talk to her was a waste of time. If I was lucky enough to hear her voice, she was monosyllabic and completely disinterested in my efforts to build a relationship. On top of that, I also discovered that the receptionist, whom I dubbed "Chatty Cathy," could not be trusted and anything I told her immediately got back to my predecessor.

I finally understood what it meant to feel "lonely at the top." I was determined to do whatever it took to make things work. I would not be deterred; after all, I was now a *manager*! I put in outrageously long hours in an effort to turn things around. I was not going to be the manager who failed at this job. I was going to be successful. I was going to please my boss no matter what. Besides, I had nothing else going on in life and work seemed to fill the void. I became so obsessed with my work that there were no boundaries between my personal and professional life.

Three months passed and, although there was still no sign of the company car I had been promised, I became the dedicated slave.

The dingy, dark office space that I had forgotten about during my interview suddenly came back into view. Night after night I stayed at work alone. Sadly, the mice and cockroaches that scurried around as soon as I entered the kitchen to get my dinner out of the refrigerator made me feel less alone. But I was determined to take on the challenge of my demanding new job, doing so at my own expense. Pleasing my boss mattered more than my own sanity.

One particular evening while I was still in my office, I called my friend Grace, a fellow workaholic. She was also in her office in another part of downtown where she worked as an attorney. I complained to Grace about my plight; telling her that the company had reneged on my car deal while I slaved away day after day and night after night. We delighted in sharing our work horror stories, completely oblivious of the harm we were causing ourselves by slaving away for fourteen hours a day.

As we talked and I was completely lost in conversation, the lights on my floor suddenly clicked off. It was completely dark outside my office. I heard the elevator doors open. I was terrified and screamed "Who turned out the lights?!?" There was no response. I heard heavy footsteps coming toward my office. I imagined a large shadowy figure grabbing me, stealing me off into the night. My hands were shaking, my heart was pounding. Grace was still on the phone with me, trying to keep me calm. Keys rustled as someone opened the glass doors. The lights came back on and my heart was now in my throat. This was it, the end of the road, I was sure of it.

Then someone called out my name. I felt a wave of relief as I recognized the voice. It was our janitor. He had been in earlier and forgotten some of the equipment he needed to take to the floor below.

Grace was happy to hear that all was well. But the truth was, all was not well. *I* was not well. It was now 9:30 p.m. and it dawned on me for the first time that perhaps I should go home.

That incident, of being scared out of my wits by the janitor late at night, was the first lesson that something in my life needed to change.

The next lesson happened soon after. Although I had very few outside interests, I did occasionally indulge in a massage. One evening I arrived for an hour-long appointment. One minute I was sitting in the waiting room, the next I was lying on the floor looking up at several faces staring down at me with concern. I had passed out from sheer exhaustion.

This time the alarm bells were ringing loudly enough for me to take action; this job was now affecting my physical health. I decided I was going to quit that month—even though I had finally received my car. My manager knew that I was extremely frustrated and disappointed by the numerous false promises and kept telling me that the situation was out of his hands. Our company was part of an international conglomerate and there were many chiefs above him.

As a dedicated slave, I put up with the false promises, convincing myself each week that things would change. When I handed in my resignation, my manager and the CEO requested an exit interview. I distinctly remember the CEO saying: "Now she's leaving—we should never have given her that car!" To him the car was a reward with no reciprocity, even though I had slaved away for them. He couldn't recognize that they had reneged on the deal for months before I ever got the car!

How do you extricate yourself from an unhealthy work situation? Is it more difficult to do when you relish the challenge? Can you tell the difference between being a workaholic and a hard worker? If you are an employer, are you treating your best people with respect, or are you punishing good performance?

Workaholism—A Sanctioned Addiction

Understanding work habits today has become even more complex due to the downturn in the economy. Many people are working harder because of financial necessity. However, obligation should not be confused with compulsion or addiction. Research indicates that Canadians and Americans are working longer hours and taking less vacation time than we did twenty years ago. Statistics Canada's General Social Survey on time use found that just over a third of Canadians consider themselves workaholics. Americans, who are renowned as one of the hardest working and most productive people of the industrialized world, are also reducing their vacation days and working longer hours. In my experience, my work dependency was as harmful as an alcoholic or drug dependency because work took priority over everything else.

In addition, I became aware of the fact that I was avoiding the truth: work was filling a void and I didn't know how else to fill it. It is difficult to know when you are crossing the line; there are times when work demands your attention and you may need to dedicate a significant amount of time to a project.

The most important thing is that *you* recognize whether this is an ongoing pattern where you are neglecting yourself and your family, or whether it a period of time in your life where the short-term sacrifice has an end-date. Only *you* can answer the question and even so, you may still not be ready to accept the answer.

I remember hearing an alcoholic describing his reaction to being pulled over by the police one night. As he was told to produce his license, his first thought was "Boy, I just have to stop driving!" I could identify with his story because I was always able to find a way to justify my behavior at work. I desired approval from my manager more than I desired spending time with friends and family. I recognized that something was wrong with this picture.

As a society, we respect hard work and sacrifice as hallmarks of success. At the opposite end of the spectrum is laziness. Many people feel the pressure of being at the lower end of the continuum for fear of being judged. Or, perhaps there is a sense of having something to prove. However, when work takes over your life, medical evidence strongly suggests that you are at far greater risk of coronary and stress-related illness.

The most important thing is that you recognize whether this is an ongoing pattern where you are neglecting yourself and your family, or whether it a period of time in your life where the short-term sacrifice has an end-date.

Establishing Boundaries

If you do identify with the behavior of a workaholic, a "lights going out" moment can transform the way you approach your career or your business. You may need several of such "moments" before the penny drops. The best approach is to establish boundaries that are not punitive.

For example, if you know that it would be better to leave work at 7:00 p.m. instead of 8:00 p.m., it may mean breaking the cycle slowly by scheduling an activity for yourself that requires you to leave. Otherwise, leaving "early" may seem overwhelming. Taking incremental steps to improve work habits can prove more effective than expecting drastic change in a hurry. Professional guidance or support groups such as workaholics anonymous are another option.

Rewarding Hard Work with More Work

Many leaders inadvertently encourage hard workers to work even more demanding schedules by rewarding their efforts with more work. This badge of honor is worn proudly, although there may be a number of unintended consequences, such as driving a workaholic to do more damage to themselves; unable to break the vicious cycle.

Celebrating high levels of productivity is one thing . . . overloading an employee with more tasks is another. By consistently recognizing the individuals who "contribute more," an employer may inadvertently create a tension in the workplace where other employees now perceive themselves as "not being good enough." This is an unhealthy cycle for any organization.

When you have a "lights going out" moment, perhaps it's time to take stock in whether you are working toward an end-date or simply working and working and working. Are you a dedicated slave or are you finding true fulfillment in your career and in your life? It is important to remember that healthy people are in healthy situations. Finding balance between work life and personal life is the key to anyone's success and well-being.

Cold-Calling Cat Woman

Eliminating the Negative Thoughts that Live Rent Free

*It would be difficult to exaggerate the degree to
which we are influenced by those we influence.*

—ERIC HOFFER

Regardless of the era or locale, when we read about economic hard
times—yet another "great recession" looming ever closer—our
fear is ignited and we portend the worst. I'm certainly just as
susceptible to this sort of "doom and gloom" thinking and
negativity as the next person, and admit I partake of the "whine
and cheese" parties from time to time, but this is a story of how
I transcended that attitude by challenging myself to go way
beyond my conventional limits and comfort zone.

It was 1991, and I found myself in a role that tested my ability to remain optimistic in the face of a downside Australian
economy. At the time, I was sales director of a cinema advertising

company in Sydney. My company had landed the rights to sell advertising on behalf of the largest cinema complex ever built in the southern hemisphere.

It was a multimillion-dollar opportunity, yet due to the economy, I didn't have sufficient staff to handle the job at hand. I was responsible for the slide advertisements that precede feature screenings in theatres (still a novelty sales tactic back then) and our ad contracts were with local retail businesses. It was the most difficult of all media to sell, especially during a time when shopkeepers were very reluctant to invest in advertising. Their priority was survival.

In addition, staff turnover was rampant as salesperson after salesperson couldn't make their quotas. I still, however, had to meet senior management expectations and make this latest business venture a success. I knew I had one option. I needed to set a positive example for my staff by getting out there and cold-calling local businesses myself.

The first call did not go well. I found myself dejected, sitting in my car in dreary strip mall parking lots in the rain, listening to my windshield wipers slap back and forth, and becoming increasingly depressed as I prayed for inspiration. "God, if you can hear me, show me what to do, anything is negotiable at this point!"

As I gazed out the misty windows at a decrepit fish 'n chips shop, I noticed a sign above a storefront that read "Costumes For Rent." I ran toward the door and, once inside, could barely contain my enthusiasm. So many costumes! A shimmering black body suit caught my attention. I tried it on and looked in the mirror. *"Holy Heart failure, Batman! Can I really do this?"*

I was instantly transformed into Cold-Calling Cat Woman! Laughing with gusto, I donned the cape, mask, and ears for good measure.

My cold-calling adventure was about to heat up. I steered my bat mobile toward the auto mall—eighteen different dealers and businesses in one location, selling every type of car accessory, new and used vehicles, several body shops under one roof . . . this was going to be fun!

I parked my car, and as my cape flapped sideways in the wind and pouring rain, I asked a mechanic in the first body shop if he could point me in the direction of the mall management office. He could barely keep a straight face as he sent me up a rickety set of stairs to a portable office. Soaking wet, I climbed the stairs and knocked on the door. It slowly creaked open to reveal a pair of piercing green eyes leering at me through horn-rimmed glasses. It was nearly 5:00 p.m. and this gentleman was in no mood for visitors.

He looked me up and down and said, "I have no idea who you are or what you want, but you have my attention." I left two hours later a with a $25,000 contract. Within a week, I sold an additional $50,000 in advertising to other local businesses.

Dumbstruck that my risk had paid off, I realized that there was nothing inherently wrong with the product I was pitching. There was something wrong with my attitude. If I wasn't enjoying the experience of meeting prospective clients and projected negativity at the outset, no wonder my sales staff and I were having difficulty closing sales.

As a result, three key teachings emerged from my adopting a movie character persona that busted the prevailing economic recession mentality and transformed fear into opportunity:

Step Out of Your Comfort Zone

There is a difference between calculated versus outrageous risk-taking. Too often we hold back from taking a risk that in reality might completely energize and reinvigorate us, whether it be pursuing a new career, starting a new business that is our true passion, or simply adopting a new approach to gaining prospective clients.

Begin by identifying the roadblocks that stand in your way; are they emotional, attitudinal, or perhaps both? Ask yourself, "What is *my* truth?" Dig deep to find your own interpretation of what rings true for you in terms of your beliefs regarding the economy, opportunity, and perceived adversity. What can you personally do to overcome these obstacles?

By stepping out of my cold-calling comfort zone, I discovered that selling could be fun. In addition, I was able to suspend my conventional sales philosophies and share this new experience with my team.

Tap Into Your Creativity to Respond Positively

The majority of our choices happen at a deep, involuntary level. The subconscious has been conditioned to respond at a faster rate than the conscious mind. Scientific research reveals that there is a 5:1 ratio of negative thoughts to positive. In other words, we are programmed to pay attention to the negative. Therefore, we need to change the pattern of our thinking in order to activate our brain to override the "typical" control-and-response mechanism.

Consider athletes who train for the Olympics. They do not allow themselves the luxury of a negative thought during their preparation. Instead, they use visualization to literally create a winning state of mind. The mental preparedness is equally as important as the physical aspect of their training.

Even though we can be consciously aware of our goals and desires, we need to re-train the part of our brain that automatically reverts to a fear-based, negative response in order to achieve a different outcome.

View Happiness at Work as a Priority

There is no greater waste of energy than getting up every morning in anticipation of spending yet another day doing something we hate. If we aren't enjoying our work, chances are we're not much fun to be around. On the other hand, when we feel inspired at work, we make a difference to our co-workers and those closest to us. Our clients also benefit when we are happy, and customer service levels improve dramatically when we feel more connected to our work.

When I changed my attitude and approach to my job as cinema advertising sales director, the bottom line changed accordingly. I felt re-energized and excited to be on the road, connecting with customers and enjoying the ride—and making more money for the company and myself than ever before.

I was thrilled with the reception I received from clients as well as the steady increase in sales, and consequently, became a far better mentor to my sales staff. Enthusiasm is truly contagious! If you are miserable in your job and still feel you aren't ready to make a job change, or financially you cannot envision taking the risk right now, realize the price you pay in terms of the physiological, psychological, and emotional consequences to your well-being.

Consider the following statistics: roughly six in ten working Americans say they are happy in their current jobs. The top drivers of workplace happiness include the personal satisfaction the job provides; feeling fortunate to have a job at all; and the job being a good fit with the employee's lifestyle. Incredibly, just fifteen percent of workers say their paycheck is the number-one factor that defines their job happiness.

"One message to workers and employers is that the paycheck isn't everything," says CEO Shawn Boyer. "While we all want to be compensated fairly for our hard work, most people won't be truly happy unless they are deriving a sense of pleasure from their work and what they are contributing to the common good of the company and society as a whole."

Taking a values-based approach to work is not only an imperative for us as individuals. Corporations, small businesses, government departments and associations who do not merely pay lip service to the adage "happy employees are the most productive" are consistently at the top of the list of organizations renowned for their outstanding workplace cultures.

Consider whether you may be blocking your own hidden entrepreneurial talents or true career aspirations. When I recognize that I am giving permission to my unconstructive thoughts to live "rent free" in my head, I am surely blocking opportunities and new possibilities.

Actions speak louder than words, and Zappos offers a great illustration. CEO Tony Tsieh took this company to $1 billion in annual sales before it was sold to Amazon in 2009. His extraordinary business success story and the work culture he created has been studied by countless organizations seeking to emulate their success.

After a very brief orientation period, Zappos will pay people $2,000 to quit. Their philosophy is all about happy, dedicated employees and happy, loyal customers. As such, if employees don't feel they fit with the company or foresee a good future for themselves, Zappos offer employees the opportunity to take "the offer" and leave to pursue other opportunities.

Consider whether you may be blocking your own hidden entrepreneurial talents or true career aspirations. When I recognize that I am giving permission to my unconstructive thoughts to live " " in my head, I am surely blocking opportunities and 1 ties.

W esire to create change is greater than your desire to repe s that yield the same results, you will be ready to let go and respond differently to the negative thoughts and influences that affect you, both consciously and unconsciously.

And, you just might end up trying on a new costume of your own. By the way, I decided to purchase the Cat Woman outfit. Why rent when you can buy? It is still one of my husband's favorites!

4

FYI

A Post-It Note Can Change Your Life

In 1994 I made a life-altering decision to immigrate to Canada. I fantasized about my new life in Canada: I imagined where I would live, where I would work, how my life would be. But the process of actually getting permanent residency was not so easy. I applied to many different Canadian embassies hoping to get an interview—a major step in the immigration process. Every time a letter arrived, I was sure that my dreams were about to come true, but then I would open the envelope and read that my application had been rejected. This happened at least a half a dozen times.

Sometimes life takes you through unexpected twists and turns, leading you in directions you never planned to take. It can seem impossible to ever get back on track, but if you pay attention to the signs, you can find your way.

As I went about my "old" life back in Australia, Canada was always on my mind. I began noticing billboards and advertisements on the back of buses promoting Canadian vacations. As I waited for news regarding my immigration status, I would run into tourists from Canada, more frequently than I ever remembered. This went on for some time. On each occasion, whether it was running into Canadians or seeing the posters, I knew these were signs that I hadn't been forgotten!

Yet, the immigration red tape was incredible, and there was no rhyme or reason as to why I was being rejected. I had piles of reference letters from people in Vancouver giving me good recommendations, but it still wasn't enough. Finally, my immigration lawyer came up with a plan to get me an interview— with the Canadian Consulate in *Mexico*. It seemed like a longshot but, just when I was about to give up hope, my lawyer called me and asked, "What are you doing on September 28?" When he told me that I was going to Mexico for an interview, I cleared my calendar. Here I was, living minutes from the Canadian Consulate in Sydney, yet I spent $3,000 and flew 8,061 miles for a ten-minute interview in Mexico City!

I prepared myself for the interview by going through a criminal background check and medical test in Sydney. I told the woman at the doctor's office to send the results of the medical exam to the Consulate in Mexico—*not* the one in Sydney. She seemed confused, so I repeated these instructions. My fate was in her hands and I so hoped she got it right.

Sure enough, when I arrived in Mexico City at the doors of the Consulate, I was told that they couldn't find my medical papers. I absolutely panicked. Was this another sign? As I sat in the waiting room of the Consulate I began to wonder if this was really meant to be. I was called to the counter where a woman stood behind a glass window. She passed some papers through the opening at the bottom of the glass and said, "Welcome to Canada!"

Finally, my dream became a reality and I was given twelve months to make my move. Now I just had to find a job. Several months prior to my departure, I wrote to the Canadian division of my Australian employer (an internationally based non-profit organization), telling them I was moving to Vancouver and wanted to work with them. Amazingly, I received a response almost immediately. They asked me to call upon my arrival. Six weeks later, I was hired.

Now, with an amazing new job to go to, it seemed as though I had all my ducks in a row.

But, within three months of my arrival in Canada, my illusions of landing my dream job in my dream country were shattered. I realized fairly quickly that the only similarity between the organization I left and the one I joined was in name only. What was it that made my experience within these two divisions so different? In a word: Management. My new CEO was a nightmare to work with.

What went wrong with my plan? I took heed of all the signs, played my cards right, was living the dream that I had manifested every day for four years. Yet I was miserable. My boss and I were not getting along and nothing seemed to go right.

As part of my job, I was responsible to attend a lot of functions for the company. These events went well into the night, sometimes until 2:00 a.m. At one particular event, one of our clients was very drunk and began making advances toward me. I was incredibly uncomfortable with the situation, so about midnight, I fled the event like Cinderella without a shoe. I was so uncomfortable, I would have left my shoes, purse, coat—anything to get out of the situation!

The next day when I returned to work I was expecting a backlash, but no one said a word to me about leaving the party early. It seemed that it hadn't been a big deal.

The tension and frustration continued at this job and I spent days and nights complaining about my wretched state to anyone who would listen. I whined to strangers, friends, co-workers about my plight. Woe was me! How could I have been so stupid to think that it would be easy moving from one country to another? That my Canadian employer would have perfect management, just like the Australian counterpart?

I continued the cycle of beating up on myself and became terribly homesick as winter hit. Somehow, I found the strength to hang in as another sign revealed itself—I had my first performance review with this company. I received mostly negative feedback on my job performance. Not only that, but my boss brought up the fact that I left that one event early . . . *nine months* after it happened! She completely blindsided me, saying that I had left the event without a word and it was completely unacceptable. I couldn't believe it! In fact, I was left speechless.

This review, this incident, served as the catalyst for change. I decided I wasn't going to put up with this anymore. As a direct result of the annual performance review, I found the momentum needed to *change myself.*

How often do we expect that the signs we are waiting for, either consciously or unconsciously, must manifest themselves positively? This idea is a fallacy. Signs take many forms. Sometimes the turning point is initially cloaked in an ugly disguise such as a negative performance review. You can't see the proverbial forest from the trees, yet everything is unfolding as it should.

Even though I was not immediately clear about what my new career would look like, my moment of truth had arrived and suddenly I was open and ready to seek new opportunities.

Two weeks after the performance review, I noticed a tiny advertisement in the business section of the daily newspaper. An international seminar company was entering the Canadian market and needed trainers for their business education programs. I knew intuitively that this was a chance of a lifetime and threw myself into pursuing it. Two hundred people attended their information session at a downtown hotel. I had to audition for the position of independent training contractor and I was hired, along with eight others.

Prior to leaving my job at the non-profit organization, I was aware that the international seminar company could not guarantee training assignments on a regular basis. Therefore, I needed to prepare myself financially for the transition to self-employment by staying put and saving money while training for my seminar projects subversively.

Five months later, on my last day of work as an employee, I had some fear about my decision. But then the mail was delivered to my office as usual and there was one particular item that caught my attention. As I opened the manila folder to read the mail for the last time before passing it on to my colleagues, I saw a flyer right on the top of the pile of mail from the international seminar company, advertising *my seminar*! My CEO, the very same person who had given me the bad performance review, had attached a post-it note to the flyer, completely unaware that I was the trainer. The note was for my colleague, Eileen. It read as follows: "Eileen, this course looks really good. I think you should go!"

As I read her note, I began to laugh. It truly was a serendipitous moment. My fear dissipated and I realized that it was ok to move on. The post-it note was the sign. It was provided exclusively for me and gave me the permission I needed to leave my job.

I will never forget the day when my former colleague, who did register for the course, showed up with the flyer in her hand (post-it note still affixed). She had no idea what my plans were when I gave my notice, as I had not told anyone in my office. As she saw my name on the big screen at the front of the seminar room, she did a double-take. Eileen was genuinely happy for me. All these years later, I have never looked back.

Here are three lessons I learned that enabled me to become unstuck from my last job as an employee:

Pay Attention to the Signs that Manifest on a Regular Basis

There are always indicators present that bear witness to your gut feeling being completely accurate. Whether you are contemplating moving on, up, or out of whatever situation applies, the evidence exists—it's just a question of recognizing how the sign is revealing itself. It may not come in a blinding flash of the obvious—a bright, flashing neon sign, as many of us would think. In fact, it may take the most unusual, subtle form, like a negative performance review.

> *There are always indicators present that bear witness to your gut feeling being completely accurate. Whether you are contemplating moving on, up, or out of whatever situation applies, the evidence exists—it's just a question of recognizing how the sign is revealing itself.*

There are literally thousands of signs occurring every day that can help you make a decision, or confirm whether or not your intention is accurate.

Here is one example that occurred while writing this chapter: My daughter-in-law had cancelled her son's registration at a kindergarten because they were moving out of the area. When she tried to enroll him at the kindergarten in the soon-to-be new neighborhood, she was told on the phone that there was no room available. However, she was driving by the school and decided to go into the office in person to enquire directly. On the same morning, one family had cancelled and another applicant had shown up without the correct I.D. for her child. *Voila!* The space appeared and our grandson will be going to his new kindergarten in the new neighborhood. Seeing the school was a sign to my daughter-in-law that she should go in and enquire in person.

"Red" May Mean "Go"

Just because the signal is "red" doesn't mean you have to obey. Of course, heeding a red-light warning is a conditioned response. However, it may not be the best choice in the heat of the moment, even though all the signs say "STOP."

The Towers Watson's 2010 Global Workforce Study of over 22,000 employees in twenty-two markets revealed that employment mobility is at a decade-long low point, and many are sacrificing career growth for a secure job. A recessionary environment exacerbates the feeling of helplessness, as many people believe that they cannot escape their situation.

During volatile economic conditions, it is no wonder you may feel stuck; taking the leap of faith when there is no safety net feels overwhelming. Yet, examples abound of entrepreneurial ideas that are flourishing during tough times. These include home-based enterprises such as virtual assistants, independent financial planning and stock market trading, baked goods and confectionary, auto repair franchises, cosmetics, web-based businesses such as website design, search engine optimization, social media experts, etc. The list goes on.

The key to entrepreneurial success is, first and foremost, developing a willingness to risk. This risk is usually related to a fear of loss—what is it you are afraid to lose? Income? Security? Benefits? Identity? Once you identify these hurdles, it's much easier to find a solution and be willing to risk.

The more you educate yourself, the less your risk. Research the buying habits of your target market, then adapt your business plan and tailor it to suit your prospective customer's finances.

Self-Doubt Is the Core of Your Fears

Boom/bust economic cycles are nothing new. Nor are the cycles of a personal nature, i.e., the inevitable peaks and valleys of life. It *is* productive to experience the "valleys." I wouldn't trade mine, even though I can say categorically that they haven't been enjoyable. Nonetheless, how do I keep growing? Challenge is an essential ingredient of leading oneself. Feeling fear is a natural emotion and only you can decide where your hunch is leading you.

When you are on the precipice of change and feel afraid, determining whether or not the fear is real or self-manufactured is the first step. It may mean doing nothing about your career, or your business, or a personal matter for now if the timing doesn't feel right. Or, it may propel you to move in a new direction.

If my job and workplace weren't going to change, *it was up to me to change.* The same can be said about every uncomfortable predicament in which I have found myself, and will inevitably continue to find myself. Staying stuck in a job or career where the situation has become untenable will invariably take a toll.

Only you can decide whether that psychological toll of staying outweighs the financial risk of leaving. As you go through the process of making up your mind, take time to come to a decision. Become aware of the sign posts that appear along the way and recognize that you can choose to view them as an obstacle or an opportunity.

As you discover new ways to re-design your path in order to lead yourself in your career, your business, and the grand scheme of your life, apply new strategies and acquire an innovative way of thinking when in a rock or a hard place.

is to detangle
order to make
ruths about
your inner

Road Worrier

The Glamour of Self-Employment

For every two minutes of glamour,
there are eight hours of hard work.

—JESSICA SAVITCH

When deciding whether self-employment is right for you, it is important to understand the challenges associated with being your own boss. We've all heard sayings like "the only place where success comes before work is in the dictionary." Although it is an overused cliché, the fact remains that many small businesses and solopreneurs fail because they mistakenly believe that self-employment provides a glamorous lifestyle. In my experience, nothing could be further from the truth.

Working in my family's retail business as a teenager certainly opened my eyes to the meaning of hard work. I watched my parents endure the trials and tribulations of staffing issues, robberies, days where there were no customers, several recessions, and, ultimately, liquidating their business to stave off bankruptcy. But that experience alone wasn't enough to prepare me for my own journey. While I gained invaluable insight into business operations, merchandising, selling, customer service, and employee/management challenges, having entrepreneurial roots did not give me the rite of passage to financial freedom. It took considerable time for me to see my business as an enterprise.

My first step to self-employment was values-based: the primary motivator was lack of fulfillment. I could have remained gainfully employed if I wanted to merely survive and make enough money to pay my rent and living expenses. But I wanted more. My decision to start my first speaking business was based primarily on lifestyle considerations, coupled with the belief that if it were a truly viable enterprise that allowed me to do what I loved, it could afford me a way of life that would be immensely gratifying. At the core, I believed in myself enough to take the risk.

If you are contemplating leaving your job or starting a new venture, your capacity to be brutally honest regarding your expectations is a good place to start. The first step requires honing an unfamiliar kind of mental toughness that will force you to personally dig deep and assess your own reality. Do you feel resentment about your current situation? How is that resentment playing out in your partnership, your family, your life? You have to be willing and ready to do this for yourself; you have to let go of fear, step into the unknown, and be prepared for all the bumps along the way.

In November 1995, I delivered my first business seminar as an independent contractor. The exhilaration I experienced afterwards was indescribable and I knew immediately that this new career was for me. As I flew out of Vancouver to Calgary and read all the seminar evaluations, I was on an emotional high. That is, until the plane landed in −20 temperatures and I had to drive a rental car on black ice along the traffic-heavy Deerfoot trail. I had never driven on ice, let alone snow. Unlike Canadians, Australians don't do ice or snow. It isn't part of our DNA.

When I finally arrived at the hotel, literally shaking from the experience, I discovered that my car had to be plugged in for the evening in order to avoid a frozen engine. I was accustomed to plugging in a hairdryer, but not a car. I had no idea what I was doing when it came to tucking my car in for the evening. To top it all off, I hadn't noticed the one-star rating for the hotel, so the adventure of life on the road was about to begin in earnest.

The temperature dropped to −30 overnight and the hotel heating didn't work well, to put it mildly. In the middle of the night, I woke up shivering uncontrollably. Had the lights been on, I'm sure I could've seen my breath! I ended up digging through my suitcase and putting on every piece of clothing I had except the suit I would wear the next day.

If you are contemplating leaving your job or starting a new venture, your capacity to be brutally honest regarding your expectations is a good place to start. The first step requires honing an unfamiliar kind of mental toughness that will force you to personally dig deep and assess your own reality.

The following morning, as I blow-dried my hair, the power went out in the entire building. I looked in the mirror and suddenly envisioned myself standing in front of 100 people at business seminar #2. My limp hair draped around my ears; I looked sad and unkempt—I was Cinderella before the ball! The panic set in and the tears began to flow.

Fortunately, the outage only lasted for about thirty minutes and I was able to finish getting dressed. I took a deep breath and headed for the hotel basement. After I got the seminar rolling, more problems began to arise. For most of the morning the heat went on and off in the meeting room and the audience complained that they were freezing and uncomfortable. I asked the staff to bring blankets in from the guest rooms so that the seminar attendees could drape the blankets around themselves for at least a little warmth.

As I continued with the seminar, looking out at the roomful of people cocooned in hotel blankets, a strange, unpleasant odor began to waft into the room. The hotel management had decided *this* was a perfect day to fumigate the lobby and the basement. Intermittent coughing began to rattle through the seminar as the assaulting smell of bug spray filled nostrils and lungs. Somehow I had to hold the attention of my audience until 4:00 pm and there was no way it was going to happen without finding a different room. As we broke for lunch, I told the banquet staff they had thirty minutes to find a new room, complete the setup, and offer some kind of compensation to avoid a calamity. Throughout this ordeal, I had to remain professional and ultimately deliver the course material.

So went my second day of self-employment. Welcome to the circus! The glamour-lifestyle-and-international-jetsetter myth was shattered in just one day, yet the show must go on. I discovered within myself the capacity to face these challenges head-on and successfully completed the seminar. And many more horrors such as this were to come.

So, are you ready for self-employment?

Walking the self-employment tightrope without a safety net is foolhardy. Even trapeze artists know better as they throw themselves in the air while dazzling the crowd. As a business owner, it is highly likely no one will catch you if you fall, and only a few people will demonstrate their adulation as you perform your death-defying acts in order to achieve your dream. Being the star attraction is not enough. You need to sell a lot of tickets for your show to succeed and you may have an entire cast to support, not just yourself.

If you want to avoid having your act turn into a sideshow, the advice in this chapter, as well as the following chapter, will help you build your business so you can be the best show in town. The simple truth is this: all of us are onstage in our own lives, each and every day. The platform of life is a privilege. If we are going to perform at our best, we need to do more than just show up in order to do justice to our individual talents.

Sustaining Yourself, Changing Outcomes

It is wonderful when you discover your passion and when work doesn't feel like work. However, passion alone won't sustain you. The key is to first discover yourself. Do you have the confidence and faith to deal with whatever the journey looks like? Are you willing to ride out the times when work isn't coming? Are you willing to re-think your approach and attitudes in order to change your outcomes?

Canadian Business recently ran the story of Allison Lickley, a twenty-seven-year-old student at McGill University's Desautels Faculty of Management. Lickley is a brilliant musician who attempted to turn her singer-songwriter talent into a business. She spent several years on the road as her own business manager and performer. She said, "The work and glamour of being a starving artist was starting to wear off. Being your own boss is tough and can be lonely."

Lickley quit the musician life on the road and is now studying for an MBA in finance. She hopes to find a career that requires both creative and analytical skills. Although she expressed no regrets regarding her time spent on the road being, in her words, "artist entrepreneur," she realized that her music will always be a professional hobby, not necessarily a career. The experience taught her about the "arts of networking, cold-calling, and time management." Lickley says she gets a kick out of how many business fundamentals she's already gleaned from managing her singing career. "It was something that wasn't financially profitable at the time," she says, "but it led to a lot of good exposure in my career."

Lickley's story is an example of one individual's career journey that is told with refreshing candor. Recognizing the learning curve associated with being one's own boss is one thing. Being able to acknowledge that one's path may require heading in a different direction than one had hoped is an example of the power of raw self-honesty.

It isn't always easy to know when the time has come to be able to say "I've given this my best shot . . . Perhaps there is something else I am meant to be doing at this moment." This is not an admission of failure. In Lickley's case, it did not signal the end of her passion as a musician. Rather, she made a clear, values-based decision.

Mindfulness

When it comes to making choices such as pursuing a new vocation or business, your most important asset is mindfulness. It is all about practicing *"Me"* management—being able to effectively manage yourself. The process begins by connecting with what truly feels right to you. Can you discern your own truth and are you able to follow through on your own values and beliefs by putting them into action, rather than rhetoric?

There were many lessons that I learned in the early years of being an independent contractor. When I first started out, there was one client who gave me a lot of work. I was so excited to have that kind of stability. But then, I began to realize that there was an expectation that my calendar was an open book and therefore I could be called, at a moment's notice, to work for however many days the contract required. In fact, it was indeed an "open" contract, which meant that although there were no guarantees regarding how much work I would be given, the assumption was that I was available for my contractor and no one else.

I became attached to *their* value system and made myself completely available to them. The more I continued to say "yes," the more I sacrificed opportunities for new work with other prospective clients in order to grow my business. This played havoc with my own personal time because I found it difficult to turn work down.

I realized that I was attached to what is called a "scarcity mindset." I so desperately wanted to be a successful solopreneur that I made myself completely available to this one client at the expense of all else. Unfortunately, I did not understand this concept nor the degree to which I had allowed this to be my code for living over a considerable period of time.

Dr. Stephen R. Covey, author of *The Seven Habits of Highly Effective People* wrote: "People with a scarcity mentality tend to see everything in terms of win-lose. There is only so much; and if someone else has it, that means there will be less for me. The more principle-centered we become, the more we develop an abundance mentality, the more we are genuinely happy for the successes, well-being, achievements and good fortune of other people. We believe their success adds to . . . rather than detracts from . . . our lives."

Many of us buy into what is perceived as "the norm": job = security; money = happiness; title = success. As a result, we experience an inner conflict as the real "me" is trying to find the way. Experience is truly the greatest teacher. As an independent contractor, my first client afforded me a deeper, richer learning—developing an inner-knowing around my own work habits and life priorities. As a result, I was able to define the core values that remain central to my business and personal life and, more significantly, to give them meaningful application.

If you are truly considering embarking on becoming an independent contractor and joining the self-employment world, it is important to examine your motives behind doing so and making sure that you understand the realities of this lifestyle. In order to succeed, you need to be ready for the thrill of the ride—it is sometimes exhilarating and sometimes terrifying. Make sure that you are flexible enough to change course if your plans don't quite work out. And always be mindful of your values. The more clarity you gain around your values and beliefs, the more effective "me" management becomes and the happier you will be with your new boss—*YOU*!

6

Money Doesn't Talk, It Swears

—BOB DYLAN

How Money Hungry Are You?

Making values-based decisions in business and life isn't always easy, even when we feel we know ourselves well. In particular, making decisions about money and finances, especially if we find ourselves at a crossroads in career or business, can be incredibly difficult. Conversations around money are often emotionally charged because our values come into play, even if we're not aware of it.

Therefore, the subject of money isn't merely about numbers, being practical, or even being logical. Going through the process of ascertaining what lies behind the rationale to leave a job or to stay, to invest or not to invest, to save or to spend is an important exercise because we discover more about what is actually driving such choices. We have learned and adapted a particular value system since childhood and it comes through as what we believe to be right and true. On a deeper level, the manner in which we justify our course of action is a reflection of our principles.

The financial-values dilemma is not only felt at an individual level. It happens in corporations on a daily basis. If you listen closely, you will hear people frequently professing values-laden statements regarding their workplace or the direction of their organization.

When I was preparing for a presentation with the leaders of a company in the financial services industry, I had a phone conversation with the CFO. He was addressing concerns regarding the impact of the recession on the company he worked for and said, "We cannot afford to shrink ourselves to glory." This comment revealed a great deal about a values clash occurring in the company. He was receiving push-back on his plans to maintain the status quo in terms of staff retention. A number of his peers were taking an ultra-cautious approach by entertaining cutbacks and terminations during a period of economic uncertainty.

The CFO's comment had an impact on me. I was learning that not everyone was ready to rise above the current challenge. When I gave my presentation, the values clash was clearly the elephant in the room, yet the senior leadership team saw it as a difference of opinion in the strategic direction of the business. It was hard for them to grasp why they couldn't get past it. This clash happens constantly in the business world because it's difficult for business owners to grasp that values play a role when there are differences in opinion.

Influences from the Past

By the time we are adults, we have already been subjected to numerous conflicting messages on the topic of money. My parents had very different attitudes around personal and business finances and it was no wonder I was often confused while navigating my own way in the world as a grown-up.

I would describe my mother as extremely cautious, although not necessarily frugal. My father was the polar opposite. Both were entrepreneurial in their own unique style. My father ran a small clothing manufacturing business and my mother worked part-time.

But that all changed in the early 70s when my father was forced to close his factory. I have very clear memories of those hard financial times; I distinctly remember my father at home in his robe, unemployed and depressed. My mother used whatever savings existed and opened a small retail clothing store, many miles away from our home. She was the sole breadwinner during this period and did everything to shield her children from the truth about their financial circumstances.

I vividly recall our outing to the Royal Easter Show that year, coming home laden with "show bags," as was the tradition. Each bag cost 10 cents, and I specifically remember feeling guilty about the number of bags we brought home. It felt like an extravagant expense at a time when my parents could ill-afford it. Although I knew my mother had saved her pennies to treat us that day, I felt sad rather than appreciative; I understood the lengths she had taken to put a smile on our faces. Self-indulgence was not in her makeup, yet she would make significant sacrifices for the sake of her family. As I have moved through life, I've come to appreciate the lengths my mother went through to give her family a little bit of happiness during a difficult financial time.

Later that year a family friend offered my father a business partnership that eventually became a business success story. He was grateful and excited to be working again and soon began letting "the good times roll." Within a year, he and his business partner opened two more stores and within three years, my father bought out his business partner. He enjoyed the thrill of the ride and was in his element when things were going well. He definitely knew how to enjoy the fruits of his labor.

In contrast, it was more difficult for my mother to celebrate the successes she achieved in her own right. She was renowned in the clothing industry for her business acumen, but she kept her sights on minding the money and giving her family stability.

These childhood experiences left an indelible impact on me in terms of witnessing the ups and downs, the trials and tribulations associated with making ends meet. I also recognized that my parents had different attitudes and values around earning, spending, and making money.

There is no doubt that these times in my past have affected my thinking regarding my business today and how to make it profitable. Arithmetic and accounting skills play a smaller role than you may think, which is just as well since math was never my best subject. Fortunately, I have acquired the financial values of both of my parents: I am a *calculated* risk-taker.

For example, every year I focus on a different facet of professional development. Several years ago I chose to put my energy and budget on developing my presentation skills. The decision was easy because I have always subscribed to the idea that no amount of marketing, selling, or promoting my services could yield significant results unless I focussed on the core; i.e., devoting time and money on honing my platform abilities.

It was time to literally "put my money where my mouth was." I knew the coach I wanted to work with, I had an idea of the financial outlay and I also knew that there would be no room for price negotiation. The person I selected had an excellent reputation and the investment made sense. She had no difficulty asking for the fee she wanted; however, I soon learned how her financial values came into play. When disclosing the fee for her services, her approach was masterful. She inquired about my keynote speaking fee and confirmed that her price was *exactly* the same. I knew that she wanted to make sure her fees were not beyond what her client would feel was affordable or reasonable.

As soon as you could say the word "speak" I was winging my way to San Francisco. Several thousands of dollars of flight and accommodation charges later, I found myself in the living room of her 1910 heritage-listed home at 9:00 a.m. one Friday morning. The following ten hours of one-on-one coaching were challenging, thrilling, and definitely memorable.

I would watch one of my presentations on video and she would stop the tape, literally every three to five seconds, to offer suggestions and corrections. This went on for hours. While some could find this daunting, I found it exhilarating. At lunchtime we sat at her dining table and my teacher elicited my most powerful, personal stories, most of which are in this book. The techniques I learned regarding the art of storytelling, enunciation, and delivery were worth every dollar. At 7:00 p.m., her driver took me back to my hotel and I was giddy with excitement.

My husband, who accompanied me on this trip, had spent the day amusing himself in the Marina District. That evening he was subjected to several hours with me rehashing every minute of my day spent with one of the best presentation-skills coaches in the world. Just like with the Royal Easter Show so many years before, I went home with "show bags"—full of book, videos, CDs—valuable goodies that I took great pleasure in consuming for years to come. This time, though, I didn't find sadness in the money spent, but rather, I felt the value of my investment—in my business and in myself.

Values Inventory

In order to determine your state of readiness in terms of taking the great financial leap towards a new career or business, it will serve you well to take a values inventory around this subject. By examining your philosophy, you will be able to gauge the impact of societal values, biases, and judgements that have potentially blocked you from making the changes needed in order for you to realize financial success, whatever that personally represents.

These questions will help you discover your own truths so you can move forward and no longer be restricted by self-limiting beliefs that have been under the surface, holding you back.

Is it possible to be completely objective regarding where one may stand on financial values, or indeed our entire values system? The challenge lies in the fact that we have all been influenced in varying degrees by the standards of others—be they family members, colleagues, or well-intended friends.

Therefore, the inventory exercise will also reveal the extent to which you have allowed yourself to be governed by accepted morals or ethics that perhaps hindered your professional and personal growth up until now. There are no "right" or "wrong" answers. Rather, your responses reflect your current position and beliefs and illuminate information regarding your personal values that my surprise you.

Values Inventory Clarification—Money

1. What does financial freedom represent to you?

   _____
   _____
   _____
   _____
   _____

2. When considering the notion of living comfortably, how much is "enough"?

_____

_____

_____

_____

_____

3. How would you describe "living beyond your means"?

_____

_____

_____

_____

_____

4. Do you subscribe to a scarcity or abundance mentality?

_____

_____

_____

_____

_____

5. Describe your spending patterns. For example, are you cautious, frugal, generous, care-free, etc?

_____

_____

_____

_____

6. Were you taught to manage your money at an early age?

_____

_____

_____

_____

_____

7. When you think of the term "financially responsible," how would you define it? What does it mean?

_____

_____

_____

_____

_____

8. What were some of the prevailing attitudes around money in your family?

_____

_____

_____

_____

_____

9. How has the recent economic volatility impacted your career? If you have not been affected directly, have you witnessed the effect on colleagues, business associates, clients?

_____

_____

_____

_____

_____

10. What images come up when you consider what it means to be "wealthy"?

_____

_____

_____

_____

_____

As you responded to these questions, what did you notice about yourself? Did the exercise engender a particular feeling? Did you experience a range of emotions, or were you neutral? By taking this values inventory, you will notice the extent to which values play a significant role in many of the financial decisions we make daily regarding our careers and businesses.

For example, when considering Question Four regarding spending patterns, one can view business expenditures either as an investment or a cost. Therefore, when your accountant presents the grand total of business expenses as part of your balance sheet each year, you will either say to yourself: "I have invested in the growth of my business" or "I have spent a lot of money." To which statement do you attribute a positive or negative connotation? When I decided to spend thousands of dollars for the trip to San Francisco to meet with the presentation-skills coach, I knew that I was investing in myself and my future business.

Whatever course of action you embark on regarding a new direction in your career or business will require a deep level of introspection and consideration. Most businesses fail because they are undercapitalized. They also fail because people plunge headfirst into their new venture without assessing their core financial values.

Values drive our thoughts, decisions, and results. To quote Robert Rue, a senior organizational change specialist: "When we honor our values, we feel alive and vital. When we ignore them, we feel forced, unnatural, out of step, and unhappy. Over time, we may feel a gradual sense of dull routine accompanied by regret for not following a different strategy. . . . It takes courage to face our authentic self and make the commitment to protect and care for that authentic self. The big, fundamental question is, 'Am I worth the effort?'"

> *Whatever course of action you embark on regarding a new direction in your career or business will require a deep level of introspection and consideration. Most businesses fail because they are undercapitalized. They also fail because people plunge headfirst into their new venture without assessing their core financial values.*

Remember to practice "me" management by ensuring that your money values are aligned with your vision. Having a nest egg is a reflection of values. Taking outrageous risk is also a reflection of values. Calculated risk-taking can provide the balance needed to invest in your business and in yourself and requires that you check in with your values along the way. Do you trust yourself to take the necessary economic risk to grow your business into a viable entity? When we truly understand that our values underpin everything about us that makes us tick, we are able to approach the crossroads with greater conviction.

Dusting Off Disappointment

Staying Positive When the Letdowns Pile Up

Our dilemma is that we hate change and love it at the same time; what we want is for things to stay the same but get better.

—SYDNEY HARRIS

At the end of my University career as a student, I had hopes and dreams in place to start a fresh new life. But the recession of the 80s had other plans for me. I faced an uncertain world that I was ill-prepared for. The truth is that many of us are never taught how to lead ourselves at work, in business, and in life. As a result, we settle for mediocrity and dissatisfaction. Why is it that so many talented, creative people stay in jobs that make them miserable? Is it because family responsibilities must come first and the financial risks associated with leaving are too great? Is it fear of the unknown, the comfort of the status quo? Or is it self-doubt, a lack of faith, trust . . . perhaps all of the above?

We have a burning desire to transform professionally and personally, to alter the course of our vocation, to let go of people and situations that no longer serve us, yet we hold back. Why?

The key to leading ourselves first in order to create change and realize our dreams lies in taking action. The emotion that drives inaction is fear. It is masked behind an array of excuses at a deeply unconscious level, yet most people do not realize its paralyzing power. Until the level of discontent becomes greater than the fear of change, many individuals stay stuck, perhaps for many years.

Underlying the excuse-making are past disappointments. These come in many forms. For example, a promotion not panning out, a business venture gone sour, a relationship that ended (either professional or personal), a proposal not being accepted, a competitor outbidding you, the economy keeps faltering and your clients cancel their orders . . . whatever the disappointment may have looked like, you ended up feeling as though the rug was pulled out from underneath you.

Then, you begin talking yourself out of your own success; giving power to your feelings of disappointment. You justify the subsequent inertia by telling yourself that you are not destined for better things. Next, you tell yourself that the hurt was too deep and it isn't worth trying again. The cycle of self-sabotage escalates and the wheels within your own mind keep spinning. Equipped with this mindset, it is impossible to lead yourself.

The solution to becoming unstuck and taking charge of yourself first lies in the *ability and willingness* to truly understand the many facets that contribute to the sum total of who you are and how you are influenced, subtly or otherwise, to maintain the status quo. Ultimately, the success you desire in your personal and professional life is governed by your own internal dialogue. This serves to debilitate, destroy, or drive you to greatness.

When you begin to understand and unravel the mystery of your life journey, the answers begin to reveal themselves. In order to lead yourself first at work, in business and in life, the first step requires the desire to gain insight into the power of your past and its impact on your present situation. This process will help you discover what is needed to alter the direction of your future.

If anyone had told me during career guidance classes in high school during the 70s that I could pursue a career as a professional speaker, not only would I never have believed it, I wouldn't have had a clue what they were talking about. Like most teenagers of my generation and at my school in particular, there was an expectation that we would all automatically know what we wanted to do with our lives by the time we entered our last year. I don't recall being taught about entrepreneurship, resiliency, and self-belief in the classroom. Those lessons came from my parents.

When you begin to understand and unravel the mystery of your life journey, the answers begin to reveal themselves. In order to lead yourself first at work, in business and in life, the first step requires the desire to gain insight into the power of your past and its impact on your present situation.

As for self-assurance, the experience of high school was a downer for the most part. Teenagers can be very cruel to one another and the impact can be soul-destroying. Puberty is not something I care to live through again. It played havoc with my hormones to such a degree that no pimple-cream product could save my skin or improve my dating prospects. I attended an all-girls school and was taunted for my physical appearance. No amount of encouragement from my parents could convince me to see myself as anything but the ugly duckling. I was never one of the "cool gang" and I did not have many friends.

My ultimate embarrassment occurred when I was twelve. I remember being in the school gymnasium for a PE class. The gym was decrepit and I hated those classes. We had to learn a particular routine that required mastering headstands. The music teacher was also present, playing the piano as an accompaniment to our exercises. I stood on my head as required, but I could not hold steady. Unable to maintain the pose, I came crashing down, landing on my back. The entire building shook on impact as I lay still, with my PE uniform over my head and my brown bloomers in full view. My classmates broke into convulsions of laughter. Needless to say, I wanted the ground to swallow me up.

As far as speaking in public, I was never a first choice for our debating team and self-confidence didn't feature on my report cards. I had to work hard for decent grades and it was a miracle that I was able to complete my final exams without having a nervous breakdown. Somehow, I managed to get into University because that was what was expected of me. Just like high school, University was no picnic. I was only seventeen when I entered my first year and recall the same awkwardness I felt in the high school gym. I was uncomfortable mingling with other students, although I did enjoy my studies. I chose Political Science as my major and completed my bachelor's degree with honors. International relations and world politics fascinated me because it was often a topic of discussion at the dinner table while growing up.

One of my professors, Dr. Elaine Thompson, ignited my passion to excel. She gave mesmerizing lectures and kept all her protégés spellbound. She would walk into the lecture hall wearing the most outlandish floppy hat, with her head held high as she positioned herself, cross-legged, on the table. She puffed on a cigarette and would frequently wave her extended cigarette holder around like a baton, in full command of her material. Her deep voice and theatrics ensured that her classes were riveting and entertaining. When I completed my degree, I had a burning desire to become a diplomat or a foreign correspondent. I was excited about the possibilities and threw myself into the process of applying for work with the department of foreign affairs.

The recession of 1981 put an end to that dream. I really had no idea about how I was going to earn a living and I definitely wasn't prepared for the challenges of resume writing, interviewing, or learning how to survive in any type of workplace. The concept of having relationships with co-workers and managers was not something I had thought about. No one had taught me about workplace dynamics, changing jobs, or exploring other career options when the recession hit.

The last place that I expected to find myself after four years of University was working at my father's clothing store. And I was one of the lucky ones. Had it not been for my family, I had no plan in place to sustain myself. I had already moved out of home and it became apparent that I would have to come back. With unemployment at record highs, great job opportunities for graduates were scarce. At the age of twenty-one, I possessed impressive academic credentials that meant nothing as I stared down the road to uncertainty. The disappointment was enormous.

How is it possible to move forward and maintain an optimistic outlook in the face of a huge letdown? Where do you turn when your hopes are dashed and a profound sense of disenchantment sets in? What happens next when you have little choice but to confront a new reality and the plans you have fail to materialize?

How do you channel your deep frustration into something constructive?

Spanish philosopher George Santayana (1863–1952), said in *The Life of Reason*: "Those who cannot remember the past are condemned to repeat it." If there is any truth to the notion that history repeats itself, then Santayana's prophetic insights are highly relevant today. There is a new generation of graduates facing even greater challenges than their predecessors who experienced recessions during the final decades of the last millennium. Known as "NINJAS," an acronym for No Income, No Job, no Assets, practicing self-reliance may be their single best option.

With record-high youth unemployment, many from this savvy, highly educated group are just as disenchanted with the new economic reality as their baby boomer parents who have been forced to re-shape their financial future and adapt to an outrageously volatile stock market.

As a global citizen within a world economy, no group is immune from the aftershocks felt from the latest "great recession." However, there is one stand-alone choice that any one of us can make at any time. When facing overwhelming frustration and disappointment that comes with the rude awakening of so many factors being out of our control, we always have the choice to lead ourselves first.

Disappointment Doesn't Mean Disaster

When disappointment happens, you can choose to reshape your point of view. Trusting that an unexpected turn of events will lead to even better possibilities *is* an alternative. Think about situations that you, or perhaps others closest to you, have faced. Their conundrum may have been a lot worse, yet they can serve as the role model you need to adjust your perspective.

Let Go of Control and Manage Your Expectations

Mastering the art of getting out of your own way in order for events to unfold in divine order doesn't come easy to control freaks. Yet, it is an essential element of self-leadership. You may never have all the answers or understand completely the rationale behind happenings that you cannot control. The process of letting go goes hand in hand with managing your expectations. This does not mean that you should stop expecting good things to happen—it means first accepting "what is" in order to formulate a new response, although there are no guarantees.

When you become overwhelmed by disillusionment and feel defeated by unpredictable circumstances, that is the precise moment to recognize your capacity to overcome despondency and begin to project different outcomes. Examples abound of people who seized opportunity in a down economy by either starting a new career or business, while others continue to either stand still or focus on escalating doom and gloom. Yes, it takes energy. However, the difference between the two approaches begins with attitude.

My greatest lessons were to be revealed through the process of stumbling, hurting, falling, dusting myself off, and then to keep going. Thankfully, a handful of people, including my parents, were exemplary role models along the way. Because of their influence, I gained invaluable insights regarding the connection between self-worth, self-leadership, and self-fulfillment.

Let Me Take You to Disneyland

Imagination in Business

One morning just after Christmas, my four-year-old grandson Cayden ran downstairs and jumped into his newly acquired pint-sized flame blue Ford F150 4×4 Rapter pickup truck. His seventeen-month-old sister followed in close pursuit as her mom seated her next to Cayden. They had previously embarked on several neighborhood adventures together, squealing with delight as their truck reached its maximum speed of five miles per hour.

This particular morning Cayden had already washed and shammied his vehicle and his new pride and joy was ready to hit the wintry streets. He decided it was time to discover a different kind of adventure. He was about to back out of the garage when he realized that something was missing. Suddenly, he got out of his truck and announced to his sister that he would be back in a moment. The journey could not begin without his map. Before you could say "Mickey Mouse," Cayden was back in a flash, armed with his newspaper flyer. As he unfolded the paper and looked down at the grocery store ad, he told his sister, "Ok, Carrera, I have the map. I am ready to take you to Disneyland!"

When my husband's daughter recounted the story to me on the telephone, I smiled as I visualized the entire scene. I wished I had witnessed that magical moment in person. For the remainder of the day I thought about the power of imagination and could not erase the smile from my face. I repeated this story to countless strangers who, like me, pictured the scene and marveled at the magic of make-believe.

Cayden did not need anything else to get where he needed to go; he took charge and got it done. How is it possible that as grown-ups we somehow learn to disregard the power of creative thought? In fact, sometimes we are dismissive, even scornful of the idea. By reclaiming this inherent gift of the flight of fantasy, we can change direction and realize endless possibilities.

All the adversity I've had in my life, all my troubles
and obstacles, have strengthened me . . .

—WALT DISNEY

Walt Disney provided the source for my grandson's inventiveness that morning. Both of my grandchildren enjoy his legacy every day as they watch the Disney channel on television and, hopefully one day soon, we will take them to the real Magic Kingdom! Disney has done more to inspire creativity, courage, and resourcefulness with both children and adults.

Disney's love for drawing at an early age morphed into one of the biggest film industry success stories of all time. His early setbacks included losing almost all his animation staff to the competition and losing the rights to one of his fictional characters, Oswald the Lucky Rabbit. As the production budget soared during the making of *Snow White and the Seven Dwarfs*, the world's first full-feature animation film made in Technicolor, Disney had to convince his wife Lillian, his brother Roy, and a highly skeptical group of loan officers at the Bank of America that their financial support, required to complete the project, would pay off.

The majority of the film industry was certain that this multi-million-dollar venture would break the Disney Studio. But as the saying goes, the rest is history. Had Disney bought into the opinions of the many naysayers he encountered along his business journey, his ingenuity would never have materialized and his vision for the world's most-renowned theme park would have been quashed. In addition, my grandson would never have thought to take his fantasy ride with his sister by his side.

How is it possible that as grown-ups we somehow learn to disregard the power of creative thought? In fact, sometimes we are dismissive, even scornful of the idea. By reclaiming this inherent gift of the flight of fantasy, we can change direction and realize endless possibilities.

Examples abound of people we know, either directly or indirectly—be they children, friends, acquaintances, or colleagues—who regularly practice living in their imagination and, as a result, have changed the course of their lives.

Many years ago I had the privilege of attending a lecture by Carl Hiebert, a self-described risk-taker extraordinaire from Waterloo, Ontario. His memorable presentation, "The Gift of Wings," was based on his life story of overcoming adversity in the form of a hang gliding accident that left him a paraplegic. After two months in the hospital, he recounted the moment when he placed a sign on his door that read *"gone flying."* A friend of Carl's took him to a farmer's field, where a single-seat ultralight aircraft was waiting: "As I buzzed the field and saw my empty wheelchair, I was overcome by this serendipitous moment. Even if I couldn't walk, I could still fly!"

Carl held his audience spellbound by telling his story to the accompaniment of incredible photographs that he took from the air. He had discovered another passion—aerial photography. He was the first person ever to fly an open-cockpit ultralight aircraft 5,000 miles across Canada, landing in Vancouver for the beginning of Expo '86. Carl has since written five more bestselling books, raising millions of dollars for charity. He has received numerous honors as one of the world's greatest philanthropists.

Think about where your "Disneyland" might be. What direction would you like to take, yet in your mind you decide "I can't get there until I have 'x'"? Have you unknowingly placed obstacles in your path? For example, do you catch yourself saying, "I want to interview for that job, however, I don't have the qualifications, so what's the point?" By convincing yourself this is the truth, your "Disneyland" will remain out of reach.

Your "map" is probably closer than you think; all you need to do is run upstairs and get it. For my grandson, there were no roadblocks. In his mind he required a map, found what he needed, and he wasn't about to talk himself out of it. Contrast this way of being with many an adult mindset: *"I don't have a map so I am not going to go!"* Instead, consider what resources are available to you now. Cayden had his map, his little truck, and his sister by his side. Carl Hiebert had his ultralight aircraft and revelled at the sight of the world beneath him. Disney took his love for drawing cartoon characters and created an empire. These are all examples of leading yourself first.

Should We Get Into or Get Out of Our Heads?

Well, the answer depends on where our head is at. In order to live in our imagination and alter our perspective, we may need to reboot the most complex human computer: our brain. We have acquired a manner of thinking and interpreting information over a particular period of time and, as a result, we have unconsciously and habitually trained the mind to react or respond to situations.

Think about how you decipher events and circumstances. Do you notice whether you are attaching a specific connotation that is detrimental to your self-worth? Are you aware of similar precedents? There is a difference between one unconstructive thought versus a pattern of reacting pessimistically. The more you pay heed to the repetitive, negative nature of your responses, the more you can begin to reframe your thoughts and create a different outcome.

Live in Your Imagination

You and I have heard countless expressions like these: "You're off your rocker"; "She's away with the pixies"; "He has a screw loose"; "They must be dreaming"; "That's the most ridiculous thing I've ever heard." Messages that sow the seed of doubt become the norm . . . to the point that it becomes natural to start questioning the power of what we can in fact create with our minds.

Can you identify an idea that has been floating around in your head regarding a venture or adventure you have been considering for a while? Now, take time out to vividly describe it on paper. Allow your thoughts to race across the page. Visualize the experience of living it, as if it were your current reality. You may notice that your thoughts transmit a physical reaction, such as a shudder, or laughter. When you envision this scenario, in this moment, it *is* your reality.

Repeat this exercise and each time you will craft a more profound picture, with greater detail, of this newly created state that has moved from your mental landscape onto the reality of the page. You can take pride in the fact that you conceived an idea and allowed your imagination to be unconstrained.

I remember applying for a job that attracted many resumes. I wondered what I could do to stand out from the crowd after my interview. The idea of designing a "certificate of persistence" came to me in a flash. I had never thought of doing something like that up until that moment, so I sent it to the company via fax to create a sense of urgency and, well . . . persistence.

The company called that same afternoon and scheduled a second interview. When I walked into the manager's office, my certificate was on his desk. He told me that receiving a "certificate of persistence" through the fax machine was priceless. I got the job, framed the certificate, and hung it on my wall as a visual reminder.

Focus on What You Want, Rather than What You Don't Want

By taking this step, you can create significant change in your perspective and in your current state of reality. Sports psychologists and world-class athletes are very familiar with this concept. It is difficult to imagine an Olympic champion approaching the starting line thinking, "Nah, I am never going to get over those hurdles." There is a synchronistic pattern to their thinking that always begins with the positive.

How many times have you heard a sentence that begins in the negative? Predictably, our thoughts will go precisely to whatever it is that we are not supposed to be thinking about. Instead, redesign the phrase in your head to start with a positive. Carl

Hiebert knew he couldn't walk, but instead of focusing on that, he decided he *could* fly.

Stop Blaming External Forces for Your Current Predicament

"This always happens to me" is a cop-out. It is easier to justify whatever quandary we may be facing with this line of thinking. The truth is that spending the energy to create a different life scenario seems too difficult only because "This always happens to me" is how we choose to see our reality.

If Disney had accepted that the Great Depression was his lot in life and that the film industry critics were right all along for thinking his dreams were outrageous, he would have manufactured a completely different version of history. Instead, he visualized success that was beyond anyone's imagination at the time. If Carl Hiebert had decided that his life would be confined to one room in a wheelchair, millions of people would never have benefitted from his charity work. If my grandson had decided that it was all too hard to go upstairs and get his map, he would not have gone on his adventure that day.

How you choose to interpret events is the most significant step in the entire process of leading yourself first. It is the ultimate deal-breaker.

Living in your imagination stimulates your creativity and allows you to live your life without boundaries. Any time you find yourself questioning or placing limitations on your creative process, remember that you have the capacity to initiate and act on your unique ideas.

Remind yourself to watch children at play; watch how they revel in the moment, creating their own cast of characters and source of entertainment. There is every reason to believe in make-believe . . . many of us did so once upon a time. It is this precise sense of wonderment that gives rise to the most extraordinary achievements we embrace as part of our lifestyle on a daily basis. Imagination is at the core of scientific and technological breakthroughs that we enjoy as consumers.

There would be no legacy of business visionaries to admire if imagination did not matter. To quote Carl Hiebert: "The only limitations we have are between our ears." Imagination is your greatest resource for inspiration and is always available whenever you choose. Simply go upstairs and get your map!

Flexing Your Resiliency Muscle

Sink or Survive

Man never made any material as resilient as the human spirit.

—BERN WILLIAMS

Growing up in the safety and security of Australia, it was always difficult for me to comprehend the situations that my parents endured. My father was imprisoned in two labor camps during and after the Second World War. My mother was a holocaust survivor; suffering the horror of Ravensbruck Concentration Camp for three years. My grandparents were murdered in the gas chambers along with many family members and millions of people.

I have no doubt that my parents' experiences had an indelible impact on my identity and perspective on life. I often recognize the legacy of endurance, tenacity, perseverance, inner strength, and willfulness that I have inherited from them. They were definitely resilient people.

When you Google the word "resiliency," you will find over 5,500,000 results. What a fascinating statistic for a word that encapsulates an essential character trait that lies at the core of every individual. What makes a person resilient? Can resiliency be taught or are some people better able to rebound from adversity than others?

There is certainly a "buzz" around the term in the business world right now, given the volatility of the economy. The rollercoaster ride of the stock market that many of us are reluctantly *enduring* creates enough nausea for us to reach out for the proverbial "airsickness bag" on a regular basis. Why do we choose to "stick it out"? Is it due to the fact that we are enjoying the ride? I don't think so. Perhaps it is because we identify with this premise: We are eternally optimistic about the future because we possess an inner-knowing based on our past risk-taking experiences; we know that, ultimately, the economy will prevail and the peaks and valleys are part of the journey. This is more than practicing blind faith. Rather, by viewing current circumstances in relationship to the past, we have already demonstrated an understanding of what it means to employ resiliency as a *habit*.

We have learned that adversity is a natural part of every aspect of our everyday lives. We know that although there are times when the discomfort is almost too much to bear, the alternative option of panic would place us in an anxiety-prone state; yielding results that could be far worse.

Resiliency is the cornerstone of our emotional and psychological survival in challenging times. We often underestimate our ability to rise above extremely difficult situations. The question of resiliency in relation to the aftermath of the terrorist attacks on September 11, 2001 was discussed at a recent meeting of the

American Psychological Association. Although there was general agreement regarding the psychological magnitude immediately following the event, there were differences in opinion regarding the long-term impact.

One psychologist commented as follows: "I think we are wired to deal with trauma . . . It's not only in the person. There's lots of other factors that determine whether (a person will) be resilient or not . . . Part of it has to do with who they are, their circumstances, the resources at their disposal, their own trauma histories. They're less resilient if they have health problems or a history of traumatic reactions, or lack economic resources."

In addition, research revealed much lower levels than the original estimates of 35% of post-traumatic stress disorder in those individuals directly subjected to the attacks. In fact, Yuval Neria, director of the Trauma and PTSD Program at the New York State Psychiatric Institute at Columbia University, says he was "surprised so many people are so resilient." Neria says "just a small proportion will develop trauma-related problems, such as PTSD, substance abuse, depression or cardiovascular disease."

The findings indicate that resiliency is innate. The degree to which we exercise emotional strength is influenced by a number of factors. One of those factors is family of origin. My parents were my greatest examples of overcoming tremendous adversity during their living years and I know that their legacy lives on in me.

My father often told stories about his life prior to and just after the Second World War. As the youngest of seven children, he was born in Hungary and grew up in the town of Nyírbátor.

His family was very poor, although his strict upbringing in an Orthodox Jewish household provided him with a strong foundation. In the Orthodox Jewish tradition, obedience to parents is a primary value. Yet, my father had the audacity to test his parents on numerous occasions. He was a risk-taker and engaged in outrageous teenage antics such as sneaking off in the middle of the night (thinking he would get away with it), only to come home to face the strictest punishment. His father would often tell him that his *chutzpah* would serve him well in his adulthood and that there was never reason to worry about his future.

It was as though these words became a self-fulfilling prophecy as my father endured tumultuous years as a prisoner of war on two occasions. First, in a forced labor camp in Hungary, only to be liberated by his future captors who placed him in a Russian prisoner of war camp until after the Second World War. He went home to discover that many members of his family had been murdered in the concentration camps.

Like many who faced the reality of a world changed forever, my father's survival skills prevailed. He immigrated to Australia in 1952, arriving with a small amount of cash and big dreams.

He soon recognized an opportunity to introduce automated knitting machines to his newly adopted country. With his hard work ethic, endearing personality, and strong sales skills, my father was able to secure the necessary financial backing to manufacture and ultimately sell the machines to the largest department stores in Australia and New Zealand. Dad was the first to introduce knitting machines to the southern hemisphere and became wildly successful with his new business venture.

Despite the horrors of war and loss everlastingly etched in his memory, he was nonetheless a risk-taker extraordinaire and entrepreneur before the words became popularized. Above all, his eternal optimism triumphed over his darkest times.

Even though he experienced numerous ups and downs in business, including the collapse of the knitting machine venture (he couldn't compete with a Japanese product that was introduced), he would always persevere. In fact, when faced with the biggest test of his personal life—the role of caregiver for my mother at the age of eighty—he rose to the occasion despite a breaking heart, witnessing her demise to the cruelty of dementia.

One of the greatest lessons I learned from my father was this: In order to rise above our challenges of any description, we need to focus on developing a resiliency mindset. It is a business and life strategy that many individuals and organizations must adopt in order to deal with adversity as well as uncertainty.

My father also taught me about the willingness to dig deep and gain strength from past experiences. We *can* overcome seemingly impossible challenges in the present by drawing upon our own inner resources.

The Willingness to Dig Deep and Gain Strength from Past Experiences

In order to rise above our challenges of any description, we need to focus on developing a mindset of *managing* rather than coping. "Getting a grip" is hardly a proactive approach! Yet, it is a business and life strategy that many individuals and organizations adopt in order to deal with adversity and uncertainty. Rather, the solution lies in the willingness to dig deep and gain strength from past experiences. We *can* overcome seemingly impossible challenges in the present by drawing upon our own inner resources.

My father was a teenager when he had to leave his financially strapped parents. He left school, worked the markets, and began learning how to deal with different types of people. His father told him, "You can live by your eyes," meaning he had an innate skill at handling people and situations. My father gained a lot of strength from that comment, keeping it in his mind through the experience in the forced labor camp and Russian camp.

Using his street smarts, good looks, and persuasive skills, he could quickly discern friend or foe. These skills enabled him to manage life in two camps as a prisoner of war. He knew who to trust and who not to trust. He found within himself the will and skill to survive.

Frame Your Reality

Ask yourself: "How do I perceive the enormity of my current challenge?" When faced with a particular conundrum that feels overwhelming, reflect on a different time in your life when you felt similar angst and were able to triumph over the situation. Realize that you can give power to either negative OR positive thoughts and you can choose to be consumed by a pessimistic attitude. By dwelling on destructive beliefs, there is no room to move forward. When we allow ourselves to be consumed by the worst-case scenario, irrationality will permeate the conscious state and, as a result, we lose perspective, clarity, and objectivity.

When my father's knitting machine business failed, he experienced sadness and disappointment. Nonetheless, he pulled himself up and faced the challenge head-on. With some imagination and *chutzpah*, he began a new business venture, which also became wildly successful. Although something in his life had failed, he knew that he could succeed, he could survive, he could lead himself into another successful enterprise.

When life hands you a challenge, focus on the triumph over a similar situation; you can use your positive attitude to overcome against all odds. My father did this time and again with his many business ventures. They would start out wildly successful, but would fail abruptly. Yet, he had a willingness to move from one venture to another; he was fearless in his willingness to keep risking.

Flex Your Resiliency Muscle

Every "test" in life will continue to serve us if we have the wisdom to view life through a lens of persistency. It may seem bizarre to consider how an individual can gain from an experience such as war or financial ruin. Yet, adversity provides an opportunity for insight. The question is whether we are able to tap into our *capacity* to look at the event in this manner. We are the sum total of all our life experiences and we can draw upon these anytime.

Consider the words of Michael Jordan: "I've missed more than 9,000 shots in my career. I've lost almost 300 games. Twenty-six times, I've been trusted to take the game-winning shot and missed. I've failed over and over and over again in my life. And that is why I succeed."

The fact that we are able to rise above a challenge is proof that our resiliency muscle can be exercised anytime.

Foster an Attitude of Gratitude

There is no exercise more powerful than making regular notation of the things we appreciate. There are many people living with adversity far greater than ours: people who are hungry, sick, lonely, or those who simply choose to stay stuck. Instead of indulging in self-pity when life has dealt you a rough deck of cards, remember what you *do* have and appreciate the good things in your life.

Living in Canada has been a dream come true, but when my parents were facing the ends of their lives, being so far from Australia was incredibly difficult. However, because my career affords me the opportunity and freedom to travel at a moment's notice, I was able to fly back to Australia on numerous occasions to help and visit my parents when they were facing life's greatest challenge. I was able to spend meaningful time with each one of them; thankful that I could fully experience being there and happy to know how much that meant to them as well.

Follow the Leader Within

Practicing self-leadership means taking charge of our attitude as well as our interpretation of events outside of our control, no matter what the circumstances. Never underestimate the power of your own imagination and resourcefulness. No matter what is against you, there is a way to overcome the odds.

As a manager, I remember how one of the most accomplished salespeople on my team during the recession of the early 1990s used to say: "there is no recession in my head." I know with certainty that had he bought into the pervading negativity of his era, he never would have built enduring relationships with his clients, nor would he have achieved unprecedented success in his field. He performed brilliantly in his job because of his unwavering belief in his own ability.

Find Opportunity in Challenging Times

As mentioned earlier, there are examples from every corner of the globe of individuals from all walks of life who overcame adversity. Their stories of dealing with the struggle of doing whatever was necessary to rise above their circumstances are testaments to the power of adopting a mindset of resiliency.

Olympic skater Joannie Rochette is a great example of this. In 2010, during the Winter Olympics in Vancouver, Rochette's fifty-five-year-old mother died suddenly of a heart attack. Two days later, Rochette was scheduled to compete. Having trained for so many years to get to the Olympics, she made the decision to take to the ice as planned. After a stunning, emotional performance, she placed third in the Olympic Women's Figure Skating Short Program. Bill Thompson, chief executive officer of

Skate Canada, said of her performance: "I watched her as she was about to skate and it looked like she was struggling emotionally. She just pulled herself together and put down a performance that I think . . . was so magical and so heroic."

I encourage you to seek out these examples for inspiration as they connect us to our own character and inner resourcefulness.

Adversity Is an Experience

Being depressed, discouraged, or disappointed at certain times is natural. Almost everything we experience on a daily basis is outside of our control; therefore it makes sense that we often feel a sense of powerlessness that can crescendo into a state of overwhelm. Adapting and/or reacting are part of the human condition.

As we have seen, tapping into our inner resolve *is* within our control. We do possess the capacity to flex our resiliency muscle and we can choose to do so, or else it will quickly atrophy. By fostering gratitude, practicing a positive attitude, and finding opportunity in adversity, you will successfully get through the tough times. In the words of Dr. Michael LeBoef: "Adversity is an experience, not a final act." Think of what is possible when you choose to live in

> *Tapping into our inner resolve* is *within our control. We do possess the capacity to flex our resiliency muscle and we can choose to do so, or else it will quickly atrophy. By fostering gratitude, practicing a positive attitude, and finding opportunity in adversity, you will successfully get through the tough times.*

your imagination and begin to channel positive energy, commitment, and belief in this direction.

10

The Fear of Success Is Bigger than the Fear of Failure

Enemy Number One

"My goodness! What would it be like if I had the life I always wanted! How would I cope if everything I desired to achieve actually came true! Wouldn't that be terrible?" This kind of self-talk is an example of someone who possesses a "fear of success." Sounds a little silly, doesn't it? While "fear of failure" is an all-too-familiar term in modern-day ethos, we don't often hear about the "fear of success." At first glance, these phrases look different, but, in fact, they have similar interpretation. It is not unusual for people to be afraid of success because of the connotations attached to the word.

The idea of success can elicit an equal, if not greater "fear" response as failure. Furthermore, many people cannot "cope" with success and, as a result, they unconsciously sabotage it. How does this happen? In order to fully embrace "me management" it is important to understand the ramifications of such thinking, as well as the rationale (or should I say the "irrational") behind it.

The fear of success is based on three factors:

1. Regard we have for ourselves (self-concept)
2. Lack of clarification in relation to success values
3. Impact of conditioning

1. Regard for Self

As discussed in previous chapters, values are derived from a variety of influences. An individual's belief system cultivates either a positive or negative self-concept. Based on the internal lens we use to view ourselves, we attribute meaning to the terms "success" and "failure."

Self-concept goes beyond being placed under the "self-esteem" umbrella. According to the Morris Rosenberg Foundation at the University of Maryland: "Self-esteem is only one component of the self-concept," which Rosenberg defines as "totality of the individual's thoughts and feelings with reference to himself as an object . . . Besides self-esteem, self-efficacy or mastery, and self-identities are important parts of the self-concept."

The work of psychologist Albert Bandura also supports this idea: "Self-efficacy is the belief in one's capabilities to organize and execute the sources of action required to manage prospective situations." In other words, if you believe in your capabilities to manage and overcome whatever life throws at you, you will find success in your life . . . however you choose to define "success."

Is it possible to achieve success when we are unknowingly sabotaging it? If you look through your internal lens, what will you find? Many of us maintain a personal belief system that keeps working against us, without understanding its origins.

Origins of self-worth

We begin formulating a concept of our own self-worth early in life. Although we evidently survived the teen years, some memories are relished, while others remain painful to recall. I was one of those teens afflicted with severe acne. My mother lived the experience with me as though it was her own; taking me from one dermatologist to another, seeking the ultimate cure.

When I was about 13 years old, we found Dr. Susie. She became intrigued with my condition; so much so that she would photograph me from every angle and then share the images with her class of undergraduates on a regular basis. I became a case study for her, and it was deeply embarrassing for me to be put on display like that. I would subsequently endure chemical peeling as well as cortisone injections, sometimes twenty to thirty per visit, in order to prevent scarring from my cystic condition. This experience was not only painful but confirmed the low opinion I already had of myself.

Is it possible to achieve success when we are unknowingly sabotaging it? If you look through your internal lens, what will you find? Many of us maintain a personal belief system that keeps working against us, without understanding its origins.

My visits to Dr. Susie continued all the way through high school, into my early twenties, reinforcing the degree of difficulty involved in overcoming my problematic skin condition. Throw into the mix my struggle with weight and you have an idea of where my level of self-esteem was during these most formative years. Pile on the messages served up by the mass media that I bought into regarding beauty and you have one pretty screwed-up young woman.

Who was I underneath the layers of pimple creams and fad diets? As you can imagine, there was an incredible amount of distortion to my self-concept. Unless I learned how to change the pattern by addressing my core beliefs based on my self-concept, this distortion would have continued to play out in my career, in my business, and in my life. I would have lived with the notion that I did not deserve success.

Possessing a negative self-concept takes many forms. What is your "acne" tale? My goal for you, as the reader, is to pay attention to the potential long-term effect that possessing a critical self-concept has on your ability to achieve success, however it manifests for you.

Experience alone is not always sufficient to teach us what we need to know in order to alter self-destructive habits. Sometimes we need to go further by seeking out appropriate help. There is no shame in admitting that despite one's own efforts to practice "me" management around changing self-perception, we may find that we cannot do it alone. There are many resources available such as literature, counseling, support groups, etc.

In order to succeed, your desire for success
should be greater than your fear of failure.

—BILL COSBY

2. Values Inventory Clarification—"Success"

Just as the word "money" is laden with values attachments, the same can be said about the word "success." In a previous chapter, we examined money values through a series of questions in order to achieve greater alignment with our career and business objectives. Self-limiting beliefs also contribute to the continued atrophy of our self-worth.

It is essential to achieve clarity around your personal, uniquely individual definition of success in order to actually *"live it."* A starting point is to look at the following statements, examine how each one resonates with you, and ask yourself if you are ready to take action to make these statements true:

a. I am solely responsible for removing the barriers that stand in the way of success in my life.

Is this statement true for you? It may be the most important question that you will ever need to answer in order to accept where you are. If you do not believe that the responsibility to *lead yourself first* underlies your goal of achieving whatever success you desire, then you still believe in fairy dust.

b. I accept that "quick fixes" don't work and it takes time to understand myself.

This should be a no-brainer. Unfortunately, many people spend thousands of dollars on quick fixes that yield nothing. The allure of short-term payoff is something that many profitable companies understand. They know that a sucker is born every minute and can reel you in when you are at your most vulnerable. Entire industries have flourished based on providing prospective customers with false promises and false hope. Who amongst us hasn't been an easy target at some point?

The tragedy of this reality is that there is no end in sight. . . . Unless you decide to wake up and realize that *meaningful, life-altering change is a long-term proposition.* Diet clubs would go out of business in a heartbeat if this was their motto!

c. I am willing to let go of unconstructive thoughts and behaviors in order to make room for positive outcomes.

The word to underline here is *"willing."* The fact that it has appeared in this book more than twenty times is intentional. Willingness in this instance means that you are favorably disposed to letting go of negative thinking to set the stage for positive results. I am not suggesting that you can literally leap for joy every minute of every day. Allowing your inner critic to surface on occasion is human. However, if it becomes a way of life and you continue to move in a downward spiral, your journey to success will become even more daunting. Experiencing feelings of despair repeatedly causes many people to simply give up.

d. I recognize that I can avail myself to new resources rather than trying to "go it alone."

When you find yourself agreeing with this statement, change *will* happen. When you back this commitment with concrete action, nothing can stop you. I do not guarantee many things, but I am sure that successful individuals from every walk of life have embraced this step. They have mentors who guide and support them, offering suggestions and advice. They do not try to do it all and are more than happy to relinquish control regarding the effort and energy expended when trying to figure it all out alone.

There are many avenues available; be they mastermind or networking groups, associations, etc. Numerous online special-interest groups have sprouted in recent years on almost any subject that comes to mind.

**e. I am capable of creating a new self-concept and
I will channel my energy in this direction.**

If you agree with this statement, you recognize there are
aspects around your self-perception that hamper your
progress. All that is required is an acknowledgement of your
capacity to look at your internal belief system. As Dr. Phil
often asks his guests : *"How's that working for you?"* This
question is powerful and, from my own experience, it is the
quintessential element of leading yourself first.

Each statement above requires scrupulous appraisal. When
you truly evaluate your perception of yourself around these
statements, you may discover that nothing short of a beliefs and
values overhaul is in order to create the momentum for change.
There is nothing wrong with such a revelation. Every person is
a work in progress and a meaningful, healthy reality check will
further your ability to manage yourself, your life, and your career.

*People with high assurance in their capabilities
approach difficult tasks as challenges to be mastered
rather than as threats to be avoided.*

—ALBERT BANDURA

3. The Impact of Conditioning

There are widely held assumptions in our society that success
and wealth are synonymous, almost interchangeable terms. It
is at the core of many a values struggle! Consider the story of
my friend Sherry, a phenomenal chef and entrepreneur in her
own right. Sherry worked in many dining establishments prior
to establishing her highly successful catering company.

After almost twenty years in the business, Sherry became disillusioned with the industry and the eighty-hour-a-week workload associated with managing staff, schedules, menus, and excruciatingly discerning clients. She found herself in a quandary: cookery was still an immensely pleasurable experience, yet the business, although profitable, no longer excited her.

Sherry found the answer. One of her staff regularly served meals for the Union Gospel Mission. Upon further investigation, Sherry discovered that she could also contribute her time and talents by preparing gourmet meals several times a year to the homeless. Her "dining with dignity" project was a huge hit and she had no difficulty recruiting volunteers, be they suppliers or servers, on every occasion.

For Sherry, "success" and "wealth" were not measured in financial terms. She sold her business and channelled her passion in a different direction; enriched by the experience of cooking and serving people in need. Sherry was able to align her personal and professional values, thereby achieving success in her own terms.

Achieving this kind of clarity regarding what success ultimately means to you will be exhilarating. You will no longer struggle, trying to conform to a definition that feels uncomfortable. Creating this state of being means you are free to choose your vocation and relationships without guilt or explanation. There need not be any burden associated with making choices that ignite your passion.

We are conditioned to think of ourselves, our values, and other people in terms of either/or. By polarizing our thoughts into society's concept of good or bad, right or wrong, etc., it becomes difficult to discern our own unique value proposition regarding work, career, family, money, success, politics, institutions, etc.

A powerful set of influencers have shaped our ideas throughout our lives, either subtly or otherwise. Examples of these influencers include our family of origin, culture, education system, religious credo, media, etc. When we are able to identify those influencers and in turn, recognize their impact, we can see our own version of the truth through a fresh set of eyes.

Now is the best time to examine what you think about yourself, to look through that internal lens and focus on how you manage your life in the world. Change any self-perceptions that are fueling a fear of success. When you have a healthy self-concept and can effectively implement your values, you will find success in your career, your business, and your life.

11

The Tall Poppy Syndrome

When Others Sabotage Your Success Plan

In Australia, there is a unique cultural notion pertaining to the meaning of success known as "The Tall Poppy Syndrome." This saying refers to the analogy of a poppy, a tall flower, and a "go-getter"-type person who is often "cut down to size" by others who are envious of their talents or achievements. Although the idea comes from Australia, it is a common practice the world over.

Most people are more than willing to give their opinions on what is best for us. It is easy to "buy into" someone else's values—even if they are light years apart from our own. When we are "others-values-based," we are attached to societal, individual, or cultural values that do not resonate at our core.

Have you ever found yourself trying to adapt to a values system that causes discomfort? Something about it doesn't feel right and you can't quite put your finger on it? Eventually, this internal struggle of trying to align your own values with another set of divergent values may cause you such distress that you either have to speak up or move on.

I found myself in this very situation when I was at the precipice of leaving my last full-time job. During an intensive presentation-skills course that was a compulsory component for my new speaking career, I met another trainee, a woman named Rose. Rose was seemingly well put together: she was immaculately dressed, wore high-fashion labels and was pencil thin. She was "picture perfect". However, she also had a grating voice and a fake laughter. She was aware of my plans to leave my existing job to become a professional presenter. I was naive when I confided in her by discussing my fears around making the decision.

> *Most people are more than willing to give their opinions on what is best for us. It is easy to "buy into" someone else's values—even if they are light years apart from our own. When we are "others-values-based," we are attached to societal, individual, or cultural values that do not resonate at our core.*

On a number of occasions during the course, Rose would say: "You don't have to leave your job," or "It's OK if you are afraid and aren't ready to leave yet." Fortunately, I was able to hear the intent behind her words and realized they were disingenuous. Rose was projecting her own values by playing on my success fears. She had no desire to see me join the ranks of our fellow presentation-course graduates because she didn't want the competition. "The Tall Poppy Syndrome" was alive and well in Canada too. Rose did me a huge favor by helping me recognize that I was indeed on the right path. Had I bought into her ideas, I may not have made the leap.

What was it about this situation that enabled me to move through my doubts and fears to plunge into my new career? I was completely ready and intuitively knew that it was the right thing to do. I saw through her thin veil of sincerity and remained focused on my goal.

On occasions, evidence of the "Tall Poppy Syndrome" at play isn't always as clear-cut as this example, especially when it involves family and friends. Of course, these are the people you trust and turn to in life, but it is important to do a "gut check" with yourself to evaluate their advice. Is it coming out of a place of concern or is it yet another case of "Tall Poppy Syndrome"? While friends and family are always well-meaning, it is important for you to identify whether or not they are being sincere.

Competition can be ugly. In business, it is a fact of life. Individuals and organizations can play a ruthless game when everything is about winning. In the workplace, backstabbing and overt bullying are commonplace. The snipers who are out there can sniff out their prey. If you do not know how to lead yourself and rise above their tactics, you will always be a victim.

How can you tell whether you are a "Tall Poppy" target? Could it be that a colleague, business associate, or client resents any opportunity for you to be successful, senses your trepidation to move forward with a new project or venture, and plays on your emotions? Or, are they displaying genuine apprehension when they express their opinion, telling you that perhaps the risk involved in your plans isn't worth it?

Unfortunately, it is true that some people we encounter are operating from a position of self-interest and are unable to support you. Stay away from these people. If you live or work with them, or cannot separate yourself from them physically, be aware of their intentions. Resentment and jealousy are powerful weapons. Your adversaries know how to wield them effectively, especially if they sense insecurity on your part.

In the case of Rose, I was able to differentiate my values from hers. It wasn't always easy, because there were times when I questioned myself. However, I realized that there was a difference between someone playing the devil's advocate versus the saboteur.

Importantly, I did not see the need to confront her, even though I knew precisely what was happening.

Pick your battles and remember that this is a central element to leading yourself first. You may be tempted to express your disappointment regarding their behavior. The higher priority is for you to move on and keep your eye on your own prize.

Lead with Your Own Values

In order to eliminate any ambiguity regarding values that are important to you, *you need a strong sense of self.* When you are leading yourself first, the process of discerning whether you are operating from another person's values instead of your own is far less complicated.

Consider the story of my colleague, Alvin Law. Alvin was one of the first thalidomide babies born in Canada. His journey is extraordinary not only because he can do virtually everything that a person with arms can do (including driving as well as playing drums) but also because of his upbringing. Alvin understands the fear of success, the importance of self-sufficiency, and the powerlessness of excuse-making. He also understands what it means to be others-values-based.

Immediately after birth Alvin was placed into an orphanage. His birth parents rejected him. However, his adoptive parents raised him to never think of himself as different. His parents loved him the way he was and from that foundation he has enjoyed tremendous success in his professional and personal life. Above all, he believes that by learning to control your own destiny, you learn to appreciate what you have.

Alvin possesses the healthiest self-concept of any person I have encountered. Why? Alvin's mother did not take a "Pollyanna approach." To quote Alvin precisely, his mother instilled in him the following philosophies:

1. "Learn the power of adapting; most of the answers come from inside yourself."
2. "There was only one area of life that I could predict, and that was how I would react to how I was going to handle things."

Alvin landed a role in a movie called *Tiger Tom* after a producer searched the world over for someone to play the title role. The screenplay was based on the true story about a man who was mauled by a tiger in a circus and as a result, lost his arms. A once-upon-a-time highly successful person, "Tiger," became a homeless drunk living on the streets of Ireland.

Alvin was required to immerse himself in this character, so he set out into the streets to play the role. He dressed in dishevelled clothing and swaggered around as if inebriated. He looked every bit the part of the "Tiger" in his later years.

As Alvin stumbled through the city streets, he was able to experience society's reaction toward his pitiful character. As he weaved down the sidewalk, sometimes falling down, he was able to watch the reactions of passersby. He realized that, depending on how he acted, it was possible to control the "revulsion" of those around him. He described the scenario as "a perfect example of how one can control their own environment . . . what most people don't realize is that this type of control can be liberating."

Alvin's example is fascinating because he is a confident, successful entrepreneur; the antithesis of his movie character. When Alvin talks about success, he says, "(I am) not as afraid as I used to be, as I understand what it looks like now that I have experienced it. People see pressure that comes from their impression of successful people . . . they don't give off a good vibe. I don't want to be like that."

Being comfortable with success is a great place to be. For Alvin, speaking over 150 times a year has made him very successful financially as an in-demand public speaker. He describes his journey as "hard work, dedication, and sacrifice. It takes a long time to get to where you want to be and many people are insecure about the journey."

If you think that a big black shiny limousine is going to show up at the back door and take you to your life, think again.

—ALVIN'S DAD

Evaluating the Meaning of Success

As you reflect on Alvin's story, I invite you to respond to the following questions. They are designed to help you define your personal concept of success to ensure that you can effectively separate yourself from your fears and attachment to someone else's idea of what your success should look like. To truly do justice to your answers, consider each question by taking the time you need.

Success Values—Questions to Consider:

1. What are your personal, exclusive values around the term "success"?

   _____

   _____

   _____

   _____

   _____

2. How do you measure success?

   _____

   _____

   _____

   _____

3. How do you envision success?

   _____

   _____

   _____

   _____

4. Does the word elicit fear?

   _____

   _____

   _____

   _____

5. Do you project failure, either consciously or unconsciously, prior to embarking on a career or business idea? If "yes," describe some examples.

_____

_____

_____

_____

_____

6. What, if any, "others-values-based" notions of success have you accepted to be true?

_____

_____

_____

_____

7. Identify your primary value-influencers pertaining to the term "success."

_____

_____

_____

_____

_____

8. Are you conflicted in terms of what "success" represents to you? If so, what steps could you take to make changes?

_____

_____

_____

_____

_____

9. How have your core beliefs influenced your ideas around success?

_____

_____

_____

_____

_____

10. Do you engage in negative self-talk when things are going well? (e.g.: "I don't deserve this.")

_____

_____

_____

_____

The process of untangling "others' values" from your own is enlightening and liberating. In order to attain success in whatever endeavor you choose to pursue, taking a pragmatic approach will not suffice. The journey is multifaceted, and unless we comprehend the profound impact of our values and beliefs along the way in order to determine those that reverberate at a deeper level, the pathway to success will be thwarted by confusion and procrastination.

In the words of Alvin's Dad: *"Success doesn't come from buying a lottery ticket or blowing out a candle on your birthday cake. You're going to have a long journey, a long walk, and you are going to have to earn it every step of the way."*

According to Alvin, people can see the world in two ways, "Waking up every morning and being scared of the day, or waking up and looking forward to it." Which way would you like to live? Will you be easily influenced by how others respond to you and to your success? By evaluating your values and what you truly believe, you can experience a new level of clarity regarding major life, career, and business decisions.

12

Get Out of That Cubicle

The Art of "Me" Management

Dilbert, my silly slammer stress buster toy, sits on my desk, vying for my attention as soon as I walk into my office. I enjoy his "rant" each time I slam him, although he only has three sayings: "Get out of my cubicle!", "That's the stupidest thing I've ever heard!", and "You want it *when*??"

Dilbert came into my life long after I left my last full-time job working for one of "those" bosses we've all experienced in our lives, but his cubicle admonition echoes my own then-daily internal rants at the woman I named "Attila the Hun."

As soon as I started working for Phyllis, I knew that I had made a mistake. Her overbearing presence was foreboding and intimidating in itself; her steely glare and tight-lipped smirk (replete with hot pink lipstick) rendered her a force to be reckoned with.

It was common to arrive at the office at 8:00 a.m. to find her working away since dawn. I could smell the burnt coffee in the urn, so I knew that she had been there for many hours. Her disapproval of "late comers" was delivered silently and effectively.

Computers were a new phenomena in the workplace back then, and I felt very uncomfortable knowing that like many baby boomers of my era, I was going to have to learn how to use one. I knew I had a steep learning curve ahead of me. Even simple tasks felt overwhelming, and although Phyllis seemed willing to teach me the essentials, I intuitively knew that no matter how hard I tried, I wasn't going to grasp this skill in a hurry.

Two weeks into my new job, Phyllis scheduled a two-hour intensive session to help me learn the software. Patience was not her virtue. I was struggling to understand the program and she was becoming increasingly frustrated. After an agonizing hour of coaching, she lost it. I asked one too many questions and she began to scream, "When are you going to get this, you moron? How long am I going to have to sit here holding your hand?"

I began shaking and felt the tears welling up in my eyes. As Phyllis continued her tirade, I found the courage to stand up and walk away. Unbelievably, she followed me out of the office and into the ladies restroom. I had shut myself in a stall and was sobbing uncontrollably.

Her yelling reverberated as though we were in an echo chamber. She shouted, "Get out of that cubicle—*now!*"

Frozen with fear, I could not budge. As I cowered in my stall, I wondered if Phyllis was going to break down the door. I pictured her face. No doubt it had turned a deep shade of purple, a perfect complement to her pink lips and the fuchsia outfit that was her "signature" color and preferred shade of attire. She eventually gave up, and I heard the door to the outside of the restroom slam as she stormed out.

Phyllis didn't speak to me for the remainder of the week. The last time anyone had given me the silent treatment was at the age of ten. Needless to say, working in this environment became unbearable. The dysfunction soared to a new level and it became clear to me that I could no longer stay in my job.

Until the bathroom incident, I had no idea how I was going to extricate myself from the situation. When Phyllis shrieked, "Get out of that cubicle *now*!" little did I realize that her words would soon prompt me to assess my work situation in a new light.

It was the wake-up call I needed. This was my moment of truth, and I was ready to move on and find a job where I felt psychologically safe to express my opinions, to stand up for myself, and to be treated with respect and dignity.

It took several months to find a new job and physically move on, but I never looked back. Self-doubt was replaced by self-awareness and a sense that I truly deserved to fully enjoy my work environment. And that "new job" became my new career. Suddenly, I had the courage to live my dream and start a business of my own.

Have you ever found yourself in a similar predicament? How many times have you wanted to tell a manager or an annoying colleague to "get out of my cubicle"? Have you ever had a feeling almost immediately that you made a monumental mistake when you accepted a job, feeling uncomfortable expressing your thoughts right from the start, yet you allowed yourself to remain trapped?

However, if we simply leave a job without learning from our mistakes, they will inevitably play out again somewhere else. Versions of "Attila the Hun" are everywhere. They are simply embodied in a different character.

What we fail to realize is that these types of scenarios are a tremendous gift in our professional and personal development because they serve as moments of growth. Unfortunately, we waste a lot of emotional energy complaining about a colleague or manager's behavior to anyone who is within earshot, rather than confronting the situation in a professional manner. The meaning of the word "confront" is to face something. By taking this approach, we are leading ourselves first.

Why Don't We Confront Difficult Situations?

There are many reasons for not taking action, or more accurately, coming up with excuses. Can you identify with any of the following?

- *The person is in a senior role and I could lose my job*
- *There is no point, because nothing will change*
- *The relationship will deteriorate further*
- *Tensions will escalate*
- *It is easier to say nothing*
- *Getting another job is less complicated*
- *There are better things to do with my time*
- *It isn't really that bad*
- *Everyone else feels the same about that person anyway*
- *The other person always wins*

Each "explanation" is in reality simply a justification for continued inertia. By doing and saying nothing, you are condoning the behavior. When the opportunity presents itself to let another person know that you are uncomfortable with either the conversation or their conduct, you have the right to articulate your thoughts, regardless of their position.

The objective is for you *to take the lead without expecting anything*. Letting another person know why the issue is important to you is the most important reason for taking action. If I could turn the clock back, I would have addressed the situation with Phyllis after that fateful incident in the stall. The reason I was unable to do so was due to the fact that I lacked the confidence and skills to lead myself first. It never occurred to me that I had options available such as managing myself with polite, assertive communication.

When I resigned, I let her know that "I had learned a lot." Had I been more confident during the bathroom incident, my comments would have been these:

"Phyllis, I want to have a good working relationship with you. I know it is important for me to learn how to use the computer. There is a learning curve involved and I need time. I was uncomfortable when you raised your voice during the training session. I would prefer it if I was given time to practice on my own. I value respectful communication, therefore it is better for me to know that I can approach you if there is something about my work that concerns you, rather than my feeling ignored."

Assertive is Not Aggressive

There is a big difference between these two words, although it is not unusual for people to view them as similar. The above example is assertive, but some might still interpret those words as aggressive. Remember, it is not your job to second guess the response. When there is tension following an uneasy interlude, the first step is to give thought to your approach.

An aggressive methodology is the exact opposite—the proverbial "matching fire with fire." Also, consider the timing. If emotions are running high, the chances of escalating the conflict are greater if you act in the heat of the moment. Give yourself time to neutralize your emotions and plan your words. The language in the above scenario is an example of assertive, deliberate, non-blaming communication. Notice that there is an emphasis on *issues* rather than *personalities*. This is central to maintaining an assertive tone. The emphasis must always be on *what happened* rather than *who did it*.

Motives

Individuals who are leading themselves first in challenging conversations are not seeking to teach people lessons. It is not your business to play the role of arbiter when it comes to correcting another person's behavior. If that were the case, then the strategy would infer an aggressive rather than assertive style. By taking charge of yourself, you have no hidden agenda. You are taking a values-based approach by looking after your side of the street, and yours alone.

> *When you find your integrity and peace of mind is being challenged, leading yourself first is your first priority. The objective is to be able to walk away knowing that you can hold your head high because you have practiced self-respect and the power of personal leadership.*

I find that the biggest source of frustration and resistance to implementing this style of communication is based on *expectation*. As a result of hearing our pearls of wisdom, we want the other person to change, apologize and become respectful overnight. It is in that very moment that the seed of resentment is planted.

The alternative is to bury your head in the sand and adopt a passive mode. By spending time at either end of the spectrum (passive *or* aggressive), you are doing a disservice to yourself, especially when you are aware of alternatives that are far more productive and conducive to your personal well-being.

Letting Go of Control

As I reflect on my experience with Phyllis, I realized that letting go of the need to "make things better" was a far easier way to live life. This isn't the easiest lesson to learn. However, if the end result is a more balanced perspective in terms of how to spend emotional energy, then the educational experience of such situations is well worth it.

Imagine if people came together after a tough conversation and were able to say "Thank you for the learning moment you provided in my life." I say this tongue-in-cheek, even though my time with Phyllis was precisely that. I was not in a place where I could fully appreciate the lesson at the time, but after the fact, I was more mindful when I encountered similar interactions.

Perfectionism

We often spend more time with our work colleagues than we do with our own families. Day-to-day stress due to workload and deadlines can bring out the worst in all of us. When conflict happens, some people manage while others simply cope. Resolving conflict is an admirable goal, but there are times when this simply isn't possible.

There will be times when you reach an impasse with certain people. You may have the best intentions at heart, yet your desired outcome of a more harmonious relationship may remain elusive. We cannot achieve perfect results in every human interaction. Personality differences, values clashes, and opposing methodologies are common causes of workplace conflict.

When you find your integrity and peace of mind is being challenged, leading *yourself* first is your first priority. The objective is to be able to walk away knowing that you can hold your head high because you have practiced self-respect and the power of personal leadership.

13

The Accident

The Importance of Vulnerability and Humility

It began on a perfectly sunny Friday afternoon in November 1998. It was the beginning of summer in Australia with perfect temperatures, clear skies, and the flowers in bloom. My mother was living a typical enjoyable day in her retired life; she was driving home from afternoon errands in her beloved white Honda Civic. Suddenly, she lost consciousness and crashed into a fence in front of the apartment building where she and my father lived. The neighbors came running as soon as they heard the "boom."

In an instant, my mother had totalled her car. They found her dazed and confused. She was able to get out of the vehicle, shaken and frightened by the event that just took place, with no recollection of those moments that were frozen in time. At first, it appeared to be nothing serious, apart from the fact that the car was finished. It was extraordinary to know that she was able to walk away. Although she blacked out for only ten seconds, no one in our family could have imagined the long-term consequences of that fateful day.

On the following Monday, my mother went to the neurologist. Although it was impossible for him to predict what her future would look like, he told us the worst-case scenario: "Your mother has suffered a mini-stroke. This could be the onset of severe dementia. It will get progressively worse, perhaps slowly.

"Eventually she will be unable to speak, walk, or perform any basic tasks. She will sleep most of the day and will revert to an infantlike state. Her bodily functions will fail as her brain cells die. Nursing staff will feed her and strap her onto a stretcher for bathing. In effect, she will become a rag doll, propped up in a wheelchair with virtually no recollection of the past.

"In time, your mother will not recognize you as the deterioration of her mind and body takes hold."

On that sad day in November, my mother experienced the first of many episodes of multiple mini-strokes that she would endure for the next three years. The neurologist's description was unfathomable, and, sadly, completely accurate.

Over the next three years, my mother's speech and mobility deteriorated rapidly. On top of her mini-strokes, she suffered terribly from osteoarthritis. Her right hip degenerated to such an extent that the only solution was replacement surgery. My family was extremely concerned about the implications of a general anesthetic, given her deteriorating mental state. Her hip pain was so debilitating that we knew there was no choice. Although the surgery alleviated the agony, the experience sped up the onset of her dementia.

This incredibly brilliant woman who was once able to speak five languages and run her own business could no longer communicate. She would eventually be robbed of every shred of dignity, unable to fend for herself in ways that most people take for granted. All we could do was helplessly watch the illness take hold.

By April 2001, my father became my mother's official caregiver. Witnessing my father in this role was profound for a number of reasons. First, I never imagined the heartbreak of the scenario that unfolded during my parents' twilight years. Nor did my father, I am sure, imagine that he would ever find himself in the role of caregiver.

Secondly, the manner in which he fulfilled this duty provided me with the greatest lesson of viewing vulnerability as an asset when leading yourself first. My father was a proud man, yet he knew that he didn't have the means or the capacity to deal with the dementia demon on his own. Despite his pride, he reached out for help; tapping into all the resources at his disposal.

He fulfilled his duty with passion and purpose, swallowing his pride to do what needed to be done for my mother without question. He exemplified personal leadership in action from the time we received the news following the car accident to the time that she was admitted to what would be her final resting place at the nursing home.

How often do we consider vulnerability as strength in business and in life? My father knew that he did not have the capacity to look after my mother as her illness advanced, nor did he have the financial means. This combination was a horrible fact of life for our family.

When my mother first had to go into respite care, we were faced with the reality of her future. We left her in this place— where the stench of urine filled the hallways and rooms, where she was given a shared room and all of her belongings had to fit into two drawers and a closet, where she was surrounded by dreadfully out-of-date and worn furniture. It was our worst nightmare.

Unfortunately, my mother was still lucid enough to comprehend this nightmare as well. When we left her there the first night, we listened to her screaming and sobbing as we walked away from her room.

My father vowed right then and there that he would never leave her in a place like that for the long-term. His biggest fear was continuing to see her suffer and not find the absolute best care available. He made a commitment to my brother and me that he would do whatever was within his means to ask for help.

The *chutzpah* my father possessed from his younger years made a reappearance. With his business savvy and innate people skills, he began reaching out to the staff at the best nursing home in Sydney. He got to know *and connect with* the CEO, the CFO, the admissions staff, the director of nursing, the care attendants—in short, my father knew how to personalize his relationship with each and every one of them. In fact, the CFO was a real numbers guy and played by the rules. When someone in my father's financial position asked for admittance into this facility, there were a lot of financial hoops to jump through; his financial position had to be validated before admittance was allowed. Because of my father's personality, the CFO took an instant liking to him and sped up the process.

> *Life is full of constant challenges. Instead of building a wall around yourself to "stay strong," the greatest strength can be found by reaching out to others for help and making real connections.*

Finally, my father achieved what we were told was impossible—securing her admission to one of the best nursing homes within a matter of months following her hip surgery, despite being told that it would potentially take a year.

The nursing home invited new residents and their families to a morning tea with the CEO and senior staff who were either directly or indirectly providing care. As we sat in the living room on that sunny Saturday morning, looking through the windows facing the massive gardens, I noticed residents in large armchairs with wheels attached, accompanied by nurse's aids. Most were sleeping. They looked like rag dolls, just as the neurologist had described three years earlier.

The CEO sensed my sadness as I tried to hide the tears. He approached me and placed a hand on my shoulder and, with his other hand on my father's shoulder, he said, "Because of your dad, you will never have to worry about your mother again." I knew that because my father recognized the need to display his own vulnerability by taking the lead, our family was able to achieve the outcome we desired for our mother's care.

Humility Is Not Humiliation

In the words of Australian army surgeon Sir Edward "Weary" Dunlop: "The ideal leader is the servant of all . . . Able to display a disarming humility, without the loss of authority." My father adopted a posture of humility in order to achieve what was best for my mother. By revealing his vulnerability in order to receive help, he demonstrated his depth of character and commitment to do the most important thing, giving my mother the care she needed even though the last thing he wanted was to be separated from his partner of almost fifty years.

Humility should not be confused with humiliation. Rather, it is an attractive human characteristic that demonstrates a level of transparency; something that is often missing in business dynamics.

Being of Service to Others

Leading yourself first sometimes necessitates placing the needs of others ahead of your own. One of the greatest benefits of helping others is the gratifying feeling you personally experience knowing you are being of service. My father was able to apply every principle he learned in business in order to help my mother because he intuitively knew how to connect with others and always possessed a leadership mindset. From the admissions staff to the CEO, he knew that the key to making the impossible possible was an unshakeable resolve to do the best he could for her. His actions demonstrated that, by serving others, *you will* be served.

My father taught me one of the greatest lessons long after I had grown up and left home. With an amazing strength of character, and a raw openness in a leadership role, he was able to exercise humility and ask for help. His vulnerability was the key to his success in taking the lead, making things happen, and getting my mother the help she needed.

Life is full of constant challenges. Instead of building a wall around yourself to "stay strong," the greatest strength can be found by reaching out to others for help and making real connections. Your vulnerability will be one of the greatest leadership qualities you can develop and will serve you well when you truly need to take the lead.

14

Book of Hugs

Showing Up No Matter What

When I planned my trip to Australia in July 2001, I was going to present a series of workshops on behalf of a U.S. client who worked in global education. However, the weekend before my first session, our family lost the battle to keep my mother at home.

Although I knew about my mother's deteriorating state, I never knew precisely when the major turning point would take place. My father, who at age eighty was her caregiver, could no longer look after her. It was a shock to come home and witness the change in my mother with my own eyes. The day before delivering my first presentation, my family admitted my mother to a nursing home.

It was the most difficult weekend that I had ever endured. Somehow I needed to find the inner strength to show up on that Monday morning and deliver the workshop entitled "Dealing with Negative Attitudes in the Workplace." I never imagined how the timing of my family tragedy could positively impact audiences around the globe, nor could I have imagined how one of these audiences would eventually serve me.

I loved presenting this workshop, although I had not written the material myself. On the third page of the workbook, I was to instruct the audience to place a checkmark next to the types of negative attitudes that were applicable to their specific workplace. On that Monday morning, I noticed that one of the attendees had checkmarked the entire list. I was curious to know how she had arrived at these conclusions and suddenly several factors dawned on me.

I wondered how human beings could decide so quickly about the behaviors of others. Were those perceptions accurate? When I asked the attendee how long she had worked at her present job, she replied: "Six weeks." The audience gasped at her answer and I was stunned at how quickly she could make judgements on people. Suddenly, I was transported to the weekend that I had just experienced with my mother, which no one at the seminar knew about. I had not planned on sharing the story, and whether one would call it divine intervention or some other "force" that entered the seminar room, I told the audience precisely what had happened to my mother and our family. My story served to illustrate a critical point regarding human interactions: Although we often think we know people, we are quick to pass judgment and, as a result, attach labels to describe them without knowing what is happening behind the scenes, in their own lives.

How often do you find yourself in a personal or business setting where you are introduced or introduce yourself and almost immediately form negative impressions? Within a matter of seconds, we develop as many as seven to ten impressions, all of which are subjective interpretations based on physical appearance, clothing, gestures, and behaviors.

Based on this information, we form opinions as to whether we want to enter into a business arrangement, personal relationship, or professional affiliation. We make such decisions arbitrarily, without knowing more about the individual or their story. We interpret their conduct based on the quick interlude and justify our opinions after a series of interactions that are rarely substantive or meaningful.

Whenever I recall the incident of the participant who indicated that everyone in her workplace displayed negative attitudes, I am reminded of this single most important question: "Do you know their story?"

For the next six weeks upon returning to Canada, I had the opportunity to work with my global education client, presenting more of the "negative attitudes in the workplace" workshops to various groups. I made one significant change to the manner in which I delivered the information on page number three. As the inevitable "check every box to negative attitudes" section appeared and more and more people were responding by placing a checkmark in nearly every single box, I began to ask audiences the question: "Do you know their story?" I would conclude the section of the workbook by referencing my personal example regarding my mother.

One afternoon during the last coffee break, several members of the audience approached me with a gift. Unbeknownst to me, they were from the Alzheimer's and Dementia Society. They presented me with a tiny book called the *Book of Hugs*. Each one of them had signed the inside and back cover, offering words of encouragement and support. As the famous Austrian psychologist Dr. Viktor Frankl once said "one need not be a servant to be able to serve." On this particular day, it was the *audience* that served me.

Looking Beyond Observable Behaviors

As you seek to understand the actions of others, maintaining perspective on the observable versus hidden explanation places you in a position to lead yourself first. By strengthening your ability to view behaviors objectively, you will develop a greater sense of open-mindedness and empathy.

By viewing undesirable behavior from an unbiased vantage point, you will find that you are in a better position to work more effectively, rather than dwelling on whatever it is about the person that you find irritating or unpleasant. In addition, personalizing the situation will only add to your angst. By examining the situation objectively, you will often discover that another person's negativity is rarely about you.

The Attractiveness of Authenticity

Some human qualities that are often perceived as weak are actually the opposite. For example, revealing a challenging aspect of your life where you experience a personal struggle can create a unique bond with another individual who has dealt with something similar.

When I subsequently shared the story about my mother and the *Book of Hugs* gift to a group of leaders in the Oil and Gas Industry, the senior VP approached me at the conclusion of my presentation and began to cry. He had just gone through the same experience of placing his mother in a care facility. By telling my own story, he felt a deeper connection to the educational message and content because it was a story he immediately related to in his own life.

My epiphany that day at the workshop in Australia connected me to the learning of my father: his vulnerability inspired me to display my own vulnerability by revealing it to the group I was teaching. Ultimately, we all are on stage in our own lives, each day. The more we expose the truth about ourselves, the more people will be drawn to working with us and hearing our message.

By "showing up," despite the challenges, becoming flexible regarding your perceptions of people and situations, and by revealing the essence of who you are, others will benefit from your efforts. Taking an unpretentious approach emanating from your character rather than your job title can create the conditions for people to identify themselves more closely with your experience.

When I received the *Book of Hugs* from the Alzheimer's and Dementia Society attendees, it had never occurred to me that there were people in the audience who could help *me*. I had not planted them in the room and I did not know that their association existed. When you step outside of your comfort zone and divulge your humanness without expecting anything in return, there will be a ripple effect beyond your imagination.

> *By "showing up," despite the challenges, becoming flexible regarding your perceptions of people and situations, and by revealing the essence of who you are, others will benefit from your efforts.*

Risk and Reward

Taking the steps outlined above involves risk. The risk lies in self-disclosure and intuitively doing the right thing—moving out of your comfort zone and exposing your vulnerability. When the going gets tough, there is a temptation to run and hide rather than face the adversity. In a society that often demands that we remain stoic—a society that views taking a humble posture as a sign of weakness—taking a lead-yourself-first approach is a bold and better move for long-term success.

How often do you admit something about yourself that displays a layer of vulnerability? Admissions like these create a new level of openness that ultimately enhance business relationships because they occur at a deeply organic and original level. Likewise, if you notice negative behavior in your workplace, instead of making a quick judgement, try to view the behavior objectively. Most likely, there is more going on than meets the eye. By operating on a more personable plane, you can impact your career, business, and personal life in a positive manner.

15

Running to Nowhere

Unfulfilled Expectations

*If you want to accomplish the goals of your
life, you have to begin with the spirit.*

—OPRAH WINFREY

I entered a period in my life where exercise became vitally important. I ran and I ran and I ran like Forrest Gump, trying to keep myself in shape. Trying to make myself happier. Why are people so fascinated by the quest to achieve physical perfection as the ultimate pursuit of happiness? At almost every turn, we hear about the benefits of exercise and living a healthy lifestyle. The plethora of information available on these two subjects alone could keep us reading for the remainder of our lives, and we would still never finish.

One may suspect that more has been written about finding the perfect diet or celebrity diet and exercise regime than scholarly works on the economy, business, spirituality, and personal development combined, which is a rather sad commentary on society's appetite for discovering meaningful tools to live a purposeful life.

Although I am a proponent of moving my body and making healthy food choices, the majority of the time, I have learned that absolutes coupled with strict rules regarding how much I should exercise or practice greater willpower will potentially drive me insane. For the better part of a quarter of my life, I lived precisely that way. I consider myself to be one example of many individuals who seek quick fixes in order to improve themselves from the outside rather than from the inside.

My attitude towards taking care of myself with a more reasonable approach to achieving a more balanced perspective overall has been years in the making. This book is not intended whatsoever as evidence that I have "arrived" . . . far from it. Rather, its purpose is to illustrate through one person's perspective that we are indeed on a journey and if we can approach the topic of personal leadership with awareness, honest self-reflection, and a willingness to create change, we can realize a greater sense of fulfillment in any area where we consider something to be missing.

Consider this saying: "Most people take aim at nothing and hit their target with amazing accuracy." Perhaps this is a somewhat harsh perspective on personal ambition, although it is fascinating to reflect on the following piece of evidence to support this idea.

Through my own research over the past fifteen years, I have asked thousands of people attending motivational presentations or educational workshops the following four questions, in succession: "Do you have life insurance?"; "Do you have a will?"; "Do you have goals, dreams, plans, and desires?"; "Do you have your goals, dreams, plans, and desires clearly defined, in your mind's eye . . . written down?"; The responses are universally as follows: Question one: 90–95%; question two: 60–70%; question three: 90–95%; question four: 5%.

Why do the majority of respondents say that they have, in effect, taken care of dying rather than living? Why do we plan for death but not for life? Going even deeper than these findings, I have discovered it is even more important to consider what truly motivates and influences us to set goals or to not set goals.

I decided to take up running when I began my quest for a slimmer, perfect self. During my first attempt to conquer the famous "City to Surf" race in Sydney, Australia, I could visualize the end result; however, I had no plan. Instead, I threw myself into a grueling series of runs, starting with the most difficult part of the course known as the "S's," a never-ending series of winding, hilly roads in the eastern suburbs that ultimately reach their peak to provide the most spectacular panoramic vistas of the world-famous Bondi Beach.

Once one has triumphed over this torturous section of the run, it is all downhill to the finish line. Unfortunately, because I had never adopted a gradual approach to prepare for the event, I found myself cramping and crawling to the end. The experience was so distressing that I was completely turned off running for many years to come.

When I revisited the idea years later, my process was completely different. I began with five-kilometer runs, then ten kilometers, to half-marathons and finally, a marathon. The key distinction between my approach to the City to Surf and the Vancouver International Marathon was not only physical; it was a major *change in mindset*.

Having dreams, plans, and desires give us momentum to create different outcomes. The law of physics states that "a body at rest tends to stay at rest while a body in motion keeps moving." There is no question that identifying what we consider to be a worthy goal provides the impetus for change. However, the goal itself is not enough.

In order to achieve whatever objective one has in mind, whether it is personal or professional, it is important to consider the reason for the goal. For long-term success, we may find that what is really necessary is an *entire rearrangement of our thoughts and motives* before setting the actual goal.

Consider the Intention Behind Your Goal

It took a considerable period of time for me to realize that the motive behind my quest to run the "City to Surf" had nothing to do with achieving a sense of personal satisfaction or pride. In fact, it wasn't even about the goal itself. I didn't take up running to cross the finish line and raise my hands in the air. There was no joy in the accomplishment. I did not derive any pleasure from the training and certainly not from the physical pain and injury I endured, which was entirely self-inflicted.

I discovered that the driving force behind my running and obsessive exercise was rooted in *punishment rather than pleasure*. I was running to burn as many calories as possible in order to lose weight as quickly as possible. I wasn't enjoying my exercise because my motivation was based on the negative rather than the positive. Clearly, if we are not enjoying the process, we will eventually give up. Invariably, the cycle of pounds lost and gained continues.

It never occurred to me that I could take up a form of exercise simply for the enjoyment factor in order to become a fitter, healthier human being, both physically and mentally. Who knew? It was liberating to become conscious of this fact. Ten years later, I joined a running group. On Sunday mornings as we prepared for our marathons or half-marathons, you would often find us running across any bridge in the city of Vancouver in the pouring rain, or even snow.

I marveled at the fact that I found this an exhilarating experience, not only because we were motivated by training for the end goal but the real joy came from the camaraderie, laughter, and conversation en route! We placed ourselves in the hands of our fearless run leaders, who led us on a different path adventure each week.

Less than 1% of the population will complete a marathon in their lifetime. I completed my first marathon in 2005, at the age of forty-five. I did not run a super-fast time and I was perfectly fine with the result. Unlike my previous exercise feats, this one was different because I approached the goal from a completely altered perspective.

Who Are You Trying to Impress?

When we aspire to attain a specific goal, we need to be clear about whom we are aiming to please. If we visualize the end result and we are not taking steps that move us closer to it, we will ultimately be out of sorts with ourselves. The feeling of discontent may not manifest for some time. Feeling the pressure to conform to another person's or societal idea of what is right for us eventually leads to frustration and resentment.

For example, whether you are planning to write a book, run a marathon, make a career change, or start a business, the choice and the responsibility to follow through with your goal is yours. I recently encountered a woman named Mary who worked in a high-pressured environment at a busy medical practice. She ran the office and, although she enjoyed her colleagues and the nature of her work, her true passion was designing and manufacturing magnificent handmade hats.

Mary showed me her website and became excited as she explained her creations. I learned that she had a deep desire to open her own store; her hats were well-sought-after items. When I asked her why she was not pursuing her dream, Mary told me that she would . . . *one day*. When I probed a little deeper, she revealed that the owner of the medical practice had an illness and she felt obligated to stay because he had grown more reliant on her to manage the business.

In addition, Mary tolerated his vitriolic temper because he was unwell and therefore "needed her." But she was also experiencing health problems of her own by allowing herself to be affected by his behavior, coupled with the stress of management responsibilities. This is an illustration of the *disease to please* in full-swing.

By delaying her own plans to expand her hat-making into a full-time business venture, Mary was sacrificing her physical, spiritual, emotional, and mental health at her boss's expense. We can be guaranteed that Mary's story is being played out in thousands of other workplaces the world over.

Procrastination and Excuse-Making Are Easier Options

Shall we talk about procrastination now or leave it for another chapter?

Joking aside, procrastination and excuse-making are two of the most common reasons for not realizing our goals. In some respects, they are actually the same thing. We procrastinate because it is a convenient excuse for not stretching ourselves, ever so slightly, out of our comfort zones. Rather than owning up to our own pattern of indecisive behavior, it often easier to play the "blame game," even if we are doing so unconsciously. In the above example, Mary "blames" her boss for not following through on her own business goals, even though she may be unaware of her rationale to justify her decision to stay put.

It is also more expedient to give up because we create unrealistic expectations within the goal-setting process itself. We often make the procedure far too complicated rather than breaking the goal down into manageable chunks—that is, establishing a series of short-term goals that connect with the long-term, larger goal. I can personally identify with this fact when I consider the progression of writing this book. By choosing to digest the concepts put forth in this chapter and consciously following these steps, we are far more likely to move closer to seeing our goals and dreams come to fruition.

Simplify the Process

The more complex and regulated the process becomes, the less likely you are to make it happen. Instead of setting yourself up for overwhelm, think about what can be achieved by taking smaller, practical bites. You will feel less daunted by the process by taking a steady, purposeful approach. Set your objectives incrementally and remember to acknowledge and praise yourself for each milestone. Slow and steady wins the race.

Be Kind to Yourself Instead of Driving Yourself

The words of legendary actor and director Konstantin Stanislavsky say it all: "At times of great stress it is especially necessary to achieve a complete freeing of the muscles." Rather than taking a coercive, grueling approach to achieving your goals, reconfigure the messages that are constantly bombarding your psyche, emanating from well-meaning friends, family, and the less-than-friendly media about what you "should" do and why you "must" do it!

By all means, challenge yourself to set a path for change, but do so in a gentle manner. Accept that one cannot turn the clock back and develop a sense of appreciation for the opportunities that are present in the "now." Align your path with the things that are important to you and choose not to dwell in the past.

Check In with Yourself

Embarking on any new "life" project requires energy and awareness. Pay attention to the reasons for your choices. For example, if you decide that you wish to pursue a different vocation, the decision requires follow-through in the form of action. Notice any resistance or hesitation along the way and ask yourself whether the initial goal still excites you. If it doesn't, realize that it is OK to let it go.

> *Accept that one cannot turn the clock back and develop a sense of appreciation for the opportunities that are present in the "now." Align your path with the things that are important to you and choose not to dwell in the past.*

If you find yourself intentionally stalling, recognize there is a possibility that you are experiencing the fear of success. Being on the precipice of achieving your goal can be uncomfortable. You may be tempted to sabotage your achievements, because you find yourself in unfamiliar territory. The breakthrough moment happens when you recognize the power of this emotion and allow it to pass.

Now is the time to ask yourself, where you are running and why? Do you have clear reasons? By evaluating, and sometimes rearranging your thoughts and motives, you will find yourself crossing the finish line with a sense of achievement and joy. You are now standing at the starting line: *ready, set . . . steady . . . then go.*

16

You Remind Me of My Ex-Wife

Your Perception Is Your Truth

We don't see things as they are . . . We see things as we are.

—ANAIS NIN

Many of us, when planning a trip to a new overseas destination, will read travel books or study maps to educate ourselves regarding a particular culture. We may watch documentaries or look at photographs to capture a sense of what we are about to experience. As a result, we expect our findings to hold true upon our arrival. We look at virtual images of popular tourist sites. We can even look at options for hotel accommodation the same way and decide, based on that snapshot, that it would be an appealing place to stay.

Someone else may be looking at the same hotel or city and decide otherwise. Yes, it may simply be a matter of personal taste, although the interesting aspect in the decision-making process is how we attach a specific meaning to these findings. What has influenced us to think *"yes, that is a beautiful place"*? We haven't actually experienced it yet, however, we have made up our minds that it is a desirable place to go. Ultimately, we want to be proven right.

Have you ever wondered why it is that people see their environment and everything in it from different perspectives? We are often convinced that what we see is the absolute truth and nothing will dissuade us from changing our opinion. We have arrived at our conclusions based on past experiences and what others have told us to be true.

We do the same thing with people. We spot someone on the other side of the room in a social or business setting; someone we may not yet know, and immediately we form impressions regarding the person. We either gravitate toward them, or we stay away. The influencers that cause us to move toward or away from are buried deep in our subconscious mind. We do not enter the room with a clean slate. The person may not have uttered a word, yet we have already determined that they *are* a certain way.

If you have ever tried online dating, then you have reacted similarly. You tell your friends "I am open to meeting someone new," yet the first step as you begin your search is to enter "filters." The list is endless—weight, height, eye color, balding ok/not ok, kids/no kids, must be under six feet two inches! There is little room for objectivity. And so it is in real life. All our initial impressions are subjective. We cannot help ourselves and we don't leave any fields open.

Can you alter your perception? Well, that depends on several factors, including the situation, the encounter, your non-judgmental attitude, and/or your locus of control. According to psychologists, the locus of control theory holds that individuals either think they are in control of their path in life (internal locus) or they feel that external forces have either hindered or helped them (external).

Several years ago I was teaching a one-day public seminar to a group of approximately 150 people. Some of the attendees were co-workers who knew each other; many were attending on their own.

The seminar was on, of all things, conflict management. I immediately got the group interacting by way of an icebreaker activity to get people energized and acquainted. The majority partook in the exercise. One person remained seated with crossed arms. Slowly, the person uncrossed his arms and proceeded to raise his fist in the air, and then his middle finger went up. I thought I was seeing things. Although I had previously witnessed this gesture from the vantage point of my car, this was the first time anyone had given me the finger in a public seminar!

> *We are often convinced that what we see is the absolute truth and nothing will dissuade us from changing our opinion. We have arrived at our conclusions based on past experiences and what others have told us to be true.*

Fortunately, the audience was preoccupied with their first exercise and did not see what happened. Of course, the finger was meant for me, so I decided to practice my father's *chutzpah* and humility; I walked over to the gentleman in question to introduce myself and find out more about his reasons for attending my course. I did not want to make any assumptions or to label his behavior. I started the conversation with an open-ended question: "What ideas are you looking for from today's seminar that will be helpful in your day-to-day work?"

His response: "I don't want to be here. I hate these seminars and I am going to leave NOW." Slightly rattled by his answer, I took a deep breath and said, "Sir, I know that today's seminar will be a great day of learning and I hope you decide to stay. However, if you wish to leave, I will respect your decision."

I walked back to the stage as the ice-breaker activity was wrapping up and the audience returned to their seats. I hadn't been speaking for more than thirty seconds when the man stood up and shouted, "I haven't finished and I want to tell you why I am leaving." I was shocked at his outburst and I knew there would be no stopping him. The audience fell silent, their attention fully upon this moment as he proceeded to pack up his belongings. He yelled, "I cannot stand your voice and I cannot look at your face for another minute, Michelle Ray!" Then, believe it or not, he said, "You remind me of my ex-wife!" Finally, he got up and left, never to return.

Could I have changed the outcome? Probably not. Does it matter? Yes, it matters because the incident provides several key learning points regarding how we perceive people and how we respond when "under fire." First of all, the incident shows that human beings have the capacity to critique others within seconds, based on mannerisms, tone of voice, or a sensory predisposition that cannot be explained.

We can take an immediate dislike toward another human being, even though we know nothing about them. Princeton's *Wordnet* defines the verb "introject" as "incorporating (attitudes or ideas) into one's personality unconsciously."

Should you experience something similar to my "ex-wife" story in your personal or professional realm, it is important to remember that you cannot alter another person's perception or expect that the person will automatically reframe their ideas about you or the situation. What you *can* do is simply allow their perception to be different than your own.

In the end, this experience gave me perfect fodder for the conflict management seminar I was teaching. I reminded the audience that you always have a choice when confronted with conflict. You can either react or respond. The outburst served as a reminder that we can't control others, but we can control ourselves.

Although I felt some discomfort, in the grand scheme of my life there were more important things that required my attention that day. I had a job to do and I was aware that my energy needed to be directed toward delivering my material to the audience. I was able to reflect on the brief verbal interaction with the participant and concluded that I had conducted myself in a professional manner by using non-defensive, positive language.

I knew that I had not violated anyone's rights and I was being true to myself. In other words, I was comfortable knowing that I had done my best and operated according to my own value system.

Imagine how much easier life would be if we could approach disagreements, arguments, or conflict escalation in a similar way. Unfortunately, when we take comments personally and subsequently react, situations quickly become unmanageable and we are unable to detach emotionally. As a result, we lose perspective regarding mutual objectives and risk straining or losing the relationship altogether. Therefore, there are several key points to remember regarding differences in perception and the ability to remain objective when confronted by another person's version of reality.

Acknowledge Instead of Argue

There are several ways you can handle such a situation: You can argue your point, or you can acknowledge differences. The latter approach will serve you best. By allowing the disparity to exist, you demonstrate open-mindedness, even though their account of the facts may not resemble yours. Instead of saying *"you're wrong,"* you can phrase your response this way: *"I understand your point of view. I see things differently."* The key is to allow for the divergence of opinion and to recognize that individuals will interpret situations based on their own frame of reference.

Spend Your Energy Wisely

In simple physiological terms, we humans are composed of bundles of energy. How we use our energy on a daily basis yields certain results. In terms of physical, mental, and emotional energy, all activity produces an energy gain or energy drain. For example, when we become angry, we experience a trigger event that starts to "make our blood boil."

A part of the brain known as the amygdala is the center for processing emotion. How we interpret the trigger event will result in the release of hormones surging through our bodies. We are literally heating up as we prepare to either "fight or flee." The impact of this hormonal flood on our central nervous system and vital organs can cause long-term damage if we repeatedly react angrily.

Therefore, we can begin to save energy by being mindful of how we *encode* and then *decode* the trigger event, whether it is situational or personal. The key is to become aware of how to decipher experiences and to realize that the meaning we attach to them will produce consequences to our well-being.

Your Perception *IS* Your Truth

Whatever we choose to see is our truth. This means that each person has a different version of reality than other people. It doesn't mean that one version is better than the other, or that one is right and the other is wrong. Difficulties arise when we attach absolutes and become inflexible. If we can get to the source of our perceptions, we will be better able to understand how we arrive at conclusions about ourselves, other people, and the world around us.

We may find that by examining our own level of acuity, we have not been allowing ourselves new possibilities and opportunities. If I had judged the gentleman at the seminar based on his body language and subsequent explanation for leaving my seminar, I would have allowed myself to get caught up in his version of reality and, as a result, I would have distracted myself from the task at hand. Instead, I realized that I could not alter his opinion about me and therefore I stayed focused on the other 149 people who were attending the seminar.

In an earlier chapter I talked about seeing others with compassion, to get to know the story behind their attitude; but what if the other person isn't willing to see you in the same light? That is where a strong internal locus of control comes in; you cannot change someone else, you can only make a choice for how you will react to the situation.

Look at Life through a Kaleidoscope

If each person interpreted behavior and situations in an identical fashion, the world would quickly become a dull place. Instead, consider looking at life through a kaleidoscope to become an "observer of beautiful forms" (the ancient Greek translation for *kaleidoscope*). We can unravel a deeper meaning behind what we *think* we see when we become more receptive to looking at life through a broader lens.

When a situation heats up and you feel your blood begin to boil, take a step back, look at the experience through this multifaceted, multicolor lens. Realize that you cannot control others' reactions to you or a situation. As French novelist Marcel Proust once said: "The voyage of discovery is not in seeking new landscapes but in having new eyes." Once you begin to see life by taking this myopic view, you will find yourself better able to detach from an emotional situation and realize that your reality *IS* your truth and, as a result, you'll be able to spend your energy and time on the aspects of life that are much more important in that moment.

17

The Piano at the Bottom of Sydney Harbour

Moving On in the Wake of Irreversible Mistakes

I will always remember the champagne corks popping in our office as soon as the announcement hit the airwaves. The radio station I worked at had just landed the biggest coup in Australian Broadcasting history. "The Voice," John Laws, who had a face for radio, had just joined our on-air lineup of radio prima donnas—oops, I mean, personalities.

We had publicized the deal with great fanfare and the advertising sales department, including me, was the happiest of all. Live ad reads by our just-hired latest superstar acquisition would sell for more than $300 per thirty-second commercial—a figure that was previously unheard of—and there was no shortage of takers.

Within a month's time we had a waiting list accumulating as testimonial after testimonial of happy advertisers got their chance to eagerly brag about the impact the Voice had on their business. We planned a party like no other and invited the "Who's Who" of the industry to an unforgettable soiree.

"Laws" rhymed perfectly with "Jaws," so it was fitting that our station decided to hold the promotional extravaganza on Shark Island, in the middle of Sydney Harbour. Our party committee spared no expense in heralding the acquisition of the multimillion-dollar man to the first commercial news-talk radio format. The invitations, designed in the shape of a shark's mouth, became a collector's item.

The big day arrived. On a perfectly warm, sunny afternoon, I met several of my clients and colleagues at Rose Bay Pier. We were to board several privately hired boats for the short journey to Shark Island. Waiting at the pier along with us was the entire Palm Court Orchestra, the entertainment highlight of our shindig. We felt our excitement build as we watched the musicians, dressed in their perfect white tuxedos, load their equipment.

We were particularly fascinated as several men wrestled the piano into ropes in order to hoist it up over the ocean onto the boat. Suddenly, the piano started tilting, straining the ropes. The piano, an exquisite antique instrument, had not been properly secured. It slipped once out of its harness and we watched in horror as half of it dangled freely over the open water; within seconds the piano slipped again and plummeted into the ocean.

Chaos ensued. Members of the orchestra began shrieking, running back and forth along the pier in their white tuxedos, but there was nothing they could do. Even if they were able to rescue the piano, it was finished. We watched as the piano slowly sank to the bottom of the harbor, its white and black keys the last of the piano to see the light of day. Bubbles filled the surface of the water after the instrument disappeared.

The orchestra faced a dilemma. Time was of the essence and there was a party to attend.

Should the show go on? A decision was finally made to move ahead, with or without the piano. The musicians were distraught and those of us who witnessed the calamity made a pact to keep quiet so as not to embarrass them.

We arrived on the island just after noon and headed for the giant party tent. The finest champagnes, wines, and aperitifs were being served as guests began to mingle and enjoy themselves, consuming copious amounts of alcohol that quickly took effect under the midday sun.

For the next hour or so, prior to lunch being served, the drunken spectacle of advertising industry people became a sight to behold. The orchestra went about their business and played on. There was only one person not partaking in any of the festivities, a man in a perfectly pressed white tuxedo who walked around aimlessly, wearing the most forlorn expression. It was, of course, the piano player.

I wondered what became of the piano player, as well as the piano. I did hear that the instrument was irreplaceable and its fate was sealed that April afternoon. It was destined to rest at the bottom of the harbor.

The timing of this calamitous event coincided with an infamous period in Australia's business history, known as the "Bottom of the Harbour"; an expression used metaphorically in reference to tax avoidance schemes of the worst kind. This scheme began in the 1970s; business owners would transfer assets from one company to another just before taxes were due. They would then sell the "failing" company to another party (thus sending it to the "bottom of the harbour"), which made it an untaxable sale. In 1980, the Australian government made illegal this practice of sending a business to the "bottom of the harbour," and in 1982, companies had to pay all back taxes owed on "bottom of the harbour" avoidance schemes. The practices of those business owners finally caught up with them.

Whether intended or unintended, many people find themselves dealing with consequences resulting from irreversible mistakes of all kinds. Either taking part in a risky tax scheme or being a piano player with an instrument sitting at the bottom of the ocean, their world has suddenly tilted and their hopes have plummeted to the bottom of their own life's harbor.

What choices do you have when your piano "sinks" and you cannot get it back? How do you manage when a colleague drops the ball with a valuable client and there is nothing that you can do to fix it? Or a project goes off the rails and cannot be saved? Or a business deal collapses and cannot be resuscitated? Maybe your career hopes disintegrate because of a corporate decision that you cannot influence? Yet, the show . . . your life . . . must go on.

My deepest "bottom of the harbour" experience came in the form of a friendship that could not be salvaged. My irreversible mistake was mixing friendship with business. I made a decision to hire a friend to help me manage my international business. At her insistence, she convinced me that it would be an ideal situation and I excitedly agreed. She could provide me with an office, staff, and above all, trust.

The business venture was a twelve-week project that ultimately proved very successful. Unfortunately, our personal/professional boundaries became blurred once I became "the boss." I did not realize at the outset that I would have preferred the role of "friend," nor did I envisage the outcome. We had not anticipated the level of discomfort that quickly developed and as a result, she did not wish to continue the friendship once the project ended, no matter how hard I tried. Although the undertaking was everything I had hoped in terms of being profitable, I paid the highest price . . . losing a valuable relationship.

This example serves to illustrate that, although I felt a profound sense of loss, I recognized several lessons I could apply for the future. Chastising myself for making the decision to employ a friend would not serve me, as I could not undo the past. However, I learned the importance of preserving personal relationships and I now consciously choose not to blend business activities and friendship. The "mistake" served me as I became clearer regarding my principles; in particular, the potential consequences of compromising friendship at the cost of doing business.

Where in your career, your business, or your life do you feel you are at the bottom of your harbor? A mistake has been made, something irreversible has taken place . . . yet the show has to go on? The ultimate question is this: How do you accept the outcome of events that are beyond your control? In situations like these, we need to remember that we have choices:

- Leave it or try to retrieve it?
- Ignore it or adapt?
- Punish the past or be proactive about the future?
- Lament or learn?
- Belabor it, bemoan it, or benefit from it?
- React or respond?
- Punitive or proactive?
- Sabotage or support?
- Hurt or help?
- Compromise or contribute?
- Avoid, apologize, or accept?

At Shark Island, the guests didn't know the piano was missing. They were unaware of the spectacle that happened prior to their arrival. So often a mistake is made, the "piano" sinks, and we assume the show has to be cancelled and we can't go on. Imagine if we handled mistakes that took place in our own lives with the grace of the piano player? If we were proactive, productive, and could move forward, other people—be they colleagues or friends—would remain oblivious to our own drama.

When you are standing at the dock of your own life, watching whatever setbacks occur that cannot be undone, it is important to exercise the power of choice.

The More You Hold onto Something Irretrievable, the Less You Are Serving Yourself (Self-Sabotage)

When I recall the effort expended trying to rescue the relationship with my friend who became a business associate, I realize that I was wasting energy. Punishing myself for the decision to take our friendship in a professional direction was not helpful. Nor was it useful wishing that the situation had not occurred. A more productive approach would have been acknowledging the loss, expressing sadness, and moving on. Admitting this to oneself is often enough. By learning to view situations such as these from a proactive versus punitive vantage point, you are practicing personal leadership.

Accept What Is beyond Your Control

The unexpected, the unthinkable, are facts of life. There are times when you can't rescue or retrieve, but the show goes on. Seemingly perfect relationships can experience an unexpected turn. People can and will disappoint or surprise you; leaving you incredulous. No one is infallible and there are times when the challenge to accept the mistake, or the ending, or the loss seems insurmountable. The alternative approach is to develop the ability to focus on what is *within* your control. Like the piano player who experienced the shocking loss of his beloved instrument, the first step may simply mean showing up, even if you don't immediately have all the answers, trusting that more options will be revealed.

Recognize the Learning Opportunity

Every choice has consequences. Sometimes we don't have contingency plans when the inconceivable occurs. In the example of my friend who became involved in my business, I had not considered the possibility of things going sour, nor the impact resulting from changing the personal dynamic of friend to manager. At the outset, we never anticipated problems, nor did we consider the possibility of harming our relationship. For me, the greatest learning that took place was the emotional cost and being mindful of not making the same mistake again. The project served as an opportunity to appreciate the value of friendship as well as being more discerning regarding the practice of hiring business associates. In addition, maintaining delineation between private and professional matters has become paramount.

Practice Self-Acceptance

In the future, if you have a piano sinking to the bottom of your harbor that was not of your making, recognize that you do not have to go down with it. Even if you caused the "sinking," can you find a way to forgive yourself? When it comes to a project succeeding or maintaining critical client relationships in order to survive financially, many people are feeling the pressure to keep their heads above water. The same is true away from work as individuals and families struggle to stay afloat. The temptation to risk and potentially slip up is higher when you are under stress. Therefore, should the unforeseen happen, can you accept the fact that you did your best?

Staying Power—Your Priceless Commodity

As I witnessed the piano slipping out of its harness and the manner in which the orchestra was able to play on and endure the mishap, I could not help but admire their staying power. Their reaction was more than a display of professionalism when their reputation was on the line. It was an example of dealing with the unexpected and subsequently rising to the occasion with dignity.

Sometimes we are called upon to deal with events not of our own making that have the potential to shake us to the core. How we choose to act offers us with the opportunity to learn the essence of our true character.

Life presents us a series of unpredictable twists and turns, highs and lows. Sometimes we are called upon to deal with events not of our own making that have the potential to shake us to the core. How we choose to act offers us the opportunity to learn the essence of our true character. Whenever you are watching your precious beautiful piano sink to the bottom of the harbor, you have the opportunity to rise above the occasion, to accept what is out of your control, and to go on with the show.

18

Why We Leave and Why We Stay

Commitment to the Workplace

How do you feel about your work environment? Are you happy or do you feel the need to move on? Workplace surveys indicate that, despite an economic slowdown, there has been a steady increase over the past two years in the number of individuals who plan to look for new job opportunities. Even if the trend reverses, the impact of workforce mobility and knowledge transfer on organizations cannot be understated. The most common reasons cited for leaving or thinking about leaving a job relate to overall job satisfaction, relationship with one's immediate manager or supervisor, and low morale.

Whether or not you are in a leadership role, you will soon discover that there are underlying reasons for turnover that are less obvious and have little to do with achieving a sense of professional fulfillment. The emotional and financial cost of employee departures, whether voluntary or otherwise, will always be significant and ongoing, despite prevailing economic conditions.

The solution lies in preventative maintenance. Organizations could avoid the burden of rehiring if they realized that much of the "pain" is self-induced. While it is true that some aspects of an employee's decision are outside of an employer's control, the most neglected area of focus in my experience relates to the *intangible workplace motivators.*

The highest priorities ought to be building an atmosphere of trust, open communication, and creating outstanding workplace relationships. Research conducted by the Conference Board indicates that in North America, job satisfaction has been on the decline for years. In all age categories, the level of satisfaction is below 50%.

If employers paid greater attention to developing a deeper understanding of the makeup of their teams, seeking to mean-ingfully improve communication, and creating more informal opportunities for people to connect and share ideas at work, a happier and more productive work atmosphere would ensue.

My first full-time job was in the media industry during the early recession of the '80s. I was excited to finally secure a job many months after completing my university degree. My mother's new, favorite radio station was advertising on the air for an administrative assistant. She heard the ad and encouraged me to apply.

Fortunately, I was successful. Although my job description was more fitting for someone seeking an entry-level position, I was happy to be working after a frustrating, year-long search. I aspired to a career in broadcast journalism and jumped at the chance to work in the industry. The radio station had recently changed its format to "news talk," the first of its kind in Australia.

I stayed at that job for over ten years and gained invaluable experience with an organization that created a culture that was the envy of the competition. The CEO was charged with a difficult task; to make the radio station profitable with a groundbreaking, risky format. When the CEO joined the company, the station was languishing on or near the bottom of the ratings ladder. So began the climb to the top. The on-air personalities became household names and work never felt like work to most of us who had the privilege of being part of the thrilling ride to #1.

Every new milestone in revenue and audience growth was repeatedly smashed for forty-eight consecutive months. The atmosphere was ongoing fun and celebration, due to the dynamic leadership of the CEO. I vividly remember his visits to my desk. He would pull up a chair and shoot the breeze at least once a week, showing genuine interest in my personal life and professional challenges. He did this with every employee (120 people), whether you worked in the newsroom, the mailroom, or the tea room.

He encouraged the same of his senior team and invented the term *"management by walking around"* before Tom Peters coined the phrase in his leadership book, *In Search of Excellence*. The board room on our floor was open every Friday at 4:00 pm for casual get-togethers and people came from every department to socialize and have fun. The on-air talent did their job and the "behind the scenes" people like me always knew that we were part of a winning team. Why did so many of us stay for so many years? In a word: "atmosphere."

Compared to many workplaces, mine was the antithesis of most that we hear about today. People felt highly motivated because they never had to second guess whether management was aware of their contribution to the overall success of the business. The workplace culture was inclusive; happiness was a critically important intrinsic and extrinsic value. I will always treasure the memories of those years.

I could not have imagined at the time how the experience would profoundly influence my current career in terms of my research and presentations on the topic of leadership and workplace morale.

In a nutshell, organizations place an enormous focus on attracting talent. However, once on board, less attention is given to creating an environment where people *want* to stay and *voluntarily* contribute to the overall goals and objectives.

In my experience of working with businesses of every description, the reason many people become dissatisfied in their jobs is because being heard, valued, and acknowledged by management and peers is an ultimately lower priority than the work itself. At all levels, everyone feels the increasing pressure of managing their daily workload. As a result, paying attention to the human element slowly becomes neglected. Yet, this is precisely the issue that necessitates the greatest consideration. In addition, it is fascinating to note this is the one area that is within an organization's control: the atmosphere within its own walls.

> *In my experience of working with businesses of every description, the reason many people become dissatisfied in their jobs is because being heard, valued, and acknowledged by management and peers is an ultimately lower priority than the work itself.*

Fast forward six years: the news-talk station was on a ratings "high" and the overall value of the total radio network grew exponentially. The owners received an offer to sell that they could not refuse. With the change in ownership came a change in leadership. Success turned on its head and the good times ended, seemingly overnight.

I began to reconfigure my purpose in my job as the changes at the top shook us all to the core. We were taken over by a company that had no experience in the media industry. The new owners proceeded to dismantle the business, restructure the management, fire people, etc. The ratings went down, along with audiences and ad revenue.

Within an eighteen-month period, everything changed and the majority of once-upon-a-time happy employees began jumping ship, including myself. For the most part, a team of satisfied employees who were not planning to leave began to re-evaluate their own position as a direct result of an unexpected business transaction.

Consider the findings of Professor Thomas W. Lee and Terence R. Mitchell's "unfolding model of turnover." Their primary research interests include *voluntary* employee turnover and workplace motivation. Professor Lee says that to look at turnover purely in terms of job satisfaction or dissatisfaction is only part of the story:

"Turnover often is triggered by a precipitating event (e.g., a fight with the boss or an unexpected job offer) that we call a 'shock' to the system ... A shock to the system is theorized to be a distinguishable event that jars an employee toward deliberate judgments about his/her job and may lead the employee to voluntarily quit. A shock is an event that generates information or provides meaning about a person's job, and then is interpreted and integrated into the person's system of beliefs and images. . . . (Leaders) must systematically address shocks and the critical role of these shocks in the voluntary turnover process."

This research indicates that, in many cases, these precipitating events and how they are managed drive the decision to stay or leave.

The "shock" factor in my job at the radio station was the

sale of the station, all its affiliates, and subsequent takeover by a company that was unfamiliar with our industry. It is important to understand the implications of such business transactions in terms of how they are managed as well as how you, as a valuable employee, deal with unforeseen changes.

When organizations don't practice preventative maintenance in these circumstances, there will be consequences in terms of management's ability to maintain high levels of employee satisfaction in order to retain motivated, talented people. There will also be consequences to you, the individual, unless you are equipped with a new awareness regarding the realities of workplace change. There are a number of myths associated with the notion of creating and maintaining a happy, productive work atmosphere that warrant further scrutiny at all levels of an organization.

Myth # 1: The Paycheck Is a Primary Motivator

Although remuneration may initially attract people to a particular job, it isn't enough to sustain interest, productivity, and engagement. In fact, money has never been at the top of the list of workplace motivators, yet is often seen as the key solution in the attraction equation. The allure associated with the overall salary package is tangible and short-term.

For leaders, providing a paycheck may be easier than finding the energy to truly connect one-on-one with everyone on a team. Moreover, when individuals say that they are at work "just for the paycheck," they are denying the existence of a fundamental intrinsic motivator—to be recognized as a person with deeper needs, as someone who wants to know that they matter in the grand scheme of their workplace. They have something valuable to offer their employer and if they are unable to tap into their unique worth, then simply "showing up at work" becomes a drudgery and an emotionally dissatisfying experience.

Myth # 2: Building in More Extrinsic Motivators Creates a Better Atmosphere

While it is true that we are all motivated by different things outside of ourselves, the more useful approach for a business in terms of achieving a highly inspired atmosphere is to pay attention to the existence of *demotivators,* as opposed to the absence of motivators. The most common demotivator includes working with chronically negative people (in management or non-management positions) who successfully drain other peoples' energy reserves.

I have found that a lack of action builds resentment amongst those who desperately want their leadership to deal with these *people* issues. Another popular belief is that by encouraging people to work longer hours in exchange for more pay (also known as overtime), people will be motivated to work harder. In effect, longer hours justify a slowdown approach to work and do very little to enhance productivity and profitability. The physiological consequences of overtime are heightened levels of stress, which are, in fact, demotivators rather than motivators.

Myth #3: Happy People Remain Satisfied and Don't Require as Much "Nurturing"

There is no doubt that contentment regarding one's workplace and job function is a desired state. However, once we have achieved a sense of fulfillment regarding our work, praise and recognition remain critical as ongoing intrinsic motivators. We all require different "strokes" in terms of being acknowledged. A wise leader will recognize those who appreciate public recognition and those who appreciate recognition privately. Validating effort and results is also an individual responsibility, no matter what our job title may be. Peer recognition is a powerful energizer that is often more meaningful than any other form of appreciation, as we often hold the opinions of our co-workers in the highest regard. Therefore, it behooves us to express admiration and applause for a job well done, regardless of our position.

Do we take a positive workplace for granted, or do we contribute to the overall atmosphere on a regular basis by utilizing the ideas discussed in this chapter? When circumstances change unexpectedly at work, having our own proactive plan of action ultimately will serve us well in terms of own career path and/or personal aspirations. For example, if we don't like a particular style of being managed, we always have a choice in terms of the decision to speak up, stay, or leave.

Whenever you find yourself out of sync with your job, finding the source of the issue can greatly increase your ability to lead yourself and take appropriate action. Has there been a recent "shock" to the system such as a change in leadership? Do you feel valued at work? Is someone else on your team bringing you down with negativity? Are you receiving the praise and recognition you deserve?

When the need arises to exercise our choices, you can take a hands-on approach rather than seeing yourself as a victim of circumstance. You don't have to remain "stuck." Instead, seek whatever means available to find the inspiration needed to take charge of your career and your professional destiny.

19

What's Your Edible Arrangement?

Detaching from Drama

I was convinced that my gift to my client would be a big hit. I had been a fan of "Edible Arrangements" for some time and was thrilled to discover that their bouquets of edible delights packaged exquisitely in a variety of assorted fruit baskets would be warmly received in time for the Holiday Season. My good intentions turned into a nightmare.

A few weeks prior to Christmas, I decided to splurge on some of my best clients. I felt it was the right thing to do. After doing business with one particular client for the past five years, I wanted to let him know how much I appreciated his business.

I did some research and found that the nearest Edible Arrangement location was approximately fifteen miles from his office. Although I teach delegation skills to others, I decided to take the edible arrangement "thank you" project on board myself, even though I was in the throes of writing this book, with self-imposed deadlines looming closer.

Admittedly, I had cut it a little close—I placed the order just a few days prior to the holiday season. In addition, my procrastination played a role in deciding whether to deliver the gift personally or secure the services of a courier for an additional expedient fee. My decision would cost me dearly in terms of my sanity, not to mention placing an invaluable relationship at risk for the sake of the additional $30 delivery fee. The aftermath weighed heavily on my mind many days after the doomed delivery of delectable delights.

On a sunny December day, three days prior to Christmas, I decided to drive out to the "nearest" Edible Arrangements store and pick up the order myself and then drop into my client's office, bouquet in hand. I was convinced that I could do the entire trip in less than three hours so I could be back at my desk to work on my book by early afternoon.

My GPS took me so far off course that I spent an additional hour stopping along the way; pulling over to call the Edible Arrangement store half a dozen times to direct me because my navigation would not pinpoint their location. When I finally arrived, I was two hours behind schedule. My anxiety levels reached peak proportions. It was a relief to eventually be on my way and I was grateful that the freezing temperature would preserve the gift basket that I had placed on the floor of my car, behind the passenger seat.

I pictured Allan's face as he received the package, taking it home to his family, and placing the arrangement as a lovely centerpiece on his Christmas dinner table. I visualized his children enjoying the chocolate-covered array of star-shaped pineapple flowers. I imagined his family marveling at the sight of the strawberries, glistening through the clear-covered wrapping paper. As long as Allan could keep the arrangement refrigerated until he got home from work, all would be fine.

I parked around the corner from his office, murmuring self-congratulatory messages as I got out of my car: *See, wasn't it worth it to drive all this way?* I was almost at the entrance when I realized that I had forgotten the accompanying Christmas card with Allan's name and address marked on the envelope. I decided to deliver the gift regardless, placing a sticky note with Allan's name onto the wrapping paper. As the elevator approached the sixth floor, I envisioned my client's reaction. At last, the moment of anticipated joy arrived.

But I could hardly believe what happened next. The receptionist informed me that Allan was out of the office and would not be back until the following day. As one of his team members, Rosa, approached and greeted me warmly, I realized that my dilemma was about to reach a crescendo. I wondered: *What do I do with this gift? Do I leave it? Do I come back tomorrow?*

Rosa took the basket out of my hands and said, "Well, Allan isn't here today so I am sure he won't mind if we share this with the staff!" As I stood with my empty hands still outstretched, I was speechless. I didn't know if it was my place to tell them what I thought they should do with the gift intended for their boss. In a moment of awkwardness, I heard myself quietly reply, "I know he would want to share it."

When Allan returned to the office the following day, he was informed of my visit and found the remainder of the Edible Arrangement in the refrigerator. He called me late morning to express his thanks for the gift and also his dismay regarding the chain of events that took place from the moment he came into work.

It seemed that he was not happy with Rosa's decision to share the basket in the office. Things continued to spiral downward with his staff as he reacted to the near-empty gift basket. He told his staff that I had intended to give the gift to him and chastised them for not contacting him first on his cell phone before opening and eating the contents.

During the course of the holiday period, the Edible Arrangement drama continued. Upon instructions from Allan, Rosa called me to apologize for opening the package as well as any embarrassment it caused. It was clear that she didn't think she had done anything wrong—she was merely sharing a perishable gift with the entire staff. The sorry saga ruminated in my mind for several weeks.

Accountability became the question of the day, the week, the month. Allan felt that his team did not take responsibility for making the decision to open the gift in his absence. His team felt that they acted appropriately by sharing the contents of a perishable item, given that their boss was out of the office. No one was willing to say how they could have done things differently.

Unfortunately, a lack of accountability is commonplace at work and in life. When it comes to conflict escalation, personality clashes, raising tension, etc., I have lost count of the number of times a client has shared examples, either personal or professional, of situations where taking ownership is the last thing on their minds. It is always the other person's fault because it is much easier to point the finger in the opposite direction.

If you find yourself in this type of dynamic with a co-worker or manager, you are doing a disservice to yourself by not taking personal responsibility for speaking your truth in order to become the best version of yourself. You are allowing yourself to get caught up in the emotionality and drama. Maybe you enjoy it? Life wouldn't be as exciting if people at work actually got along with one another, most of the time.

Many individuals become so consumed with the chaos of their workplace relationships, they lose sight of how the trouble began, what the real issues were at the outset, and are completely unwilling to admit their role, or consider that they could adopt a completely new approach. Instead, they give up and stay stuck; waiting for the other person to change, eating the Edible Arrangement alone.

As for me, I had to own my part in the Edible Arrangement story. I had to admit that I wasted energy by trying to do too much myself, running around getting lost with my useless GPS. I placed myself in a no-win situation by not sticking to my priority to remain on course that day to finish writing this book and I felt remorse over my decision not to spend the $30 to have the delivery truck drop off the basket.

"Shoulda, woulda coulda . . ." How would it serve me if I continued rehashing? *If only . . . If only the delivery guy had dropped off the package . . . if only . . .* Blah blah blah.

I made peace with myself when I understood that the arrangement would have been consumed regardless. I decided to be happy knowing that I had done the right thing by showing my appreciation for the client relationship. I had the choice: I could be satisfied with my intentions or I could spend weeks or months second-guessing myself.

Consider the Following Questions:

1. What are your options when your best intentions backfire?
2. How do you lead yourself when the unintended consequences from your goodwill gesture spirals out of control?
3. What do you do when you find yourself ensconced in other people's drama?
4. Do you apologize, buy another gift, or let it go?

Remember Your Intention

Sometimes our best intentions backfire. Ultimately, I realized that the best thing was to acknowledge the awkwardness of the moment with Allan and Rosa by having separate conversations. I listened empathetically when Rosa called to apologize and I told her that I understood her desire to do what was best in the heat of the moment. When I spoke to Allan, I explained that it was difficult for all parties to discern another course of action upon learning that he was out of the office and that my goal was to say thank you for his business. With the benefit of hindsight, everyone agreed that it was an odd and discomforting state of affairs and that my gesture in and of itself was appreciated.

When Unintended Consequences Spiral Out of Control

The key in this situation is to separate yourself from "who did it" and instead look objectively at "what happened." If your best intentions go askew, blaming yourself for whatever transpires afterwards doesn't help you or your client. Nor is it helpful to say "should have, would have, could have." What is done is done. A more useful approach is to assess the situation and recognize what you learned about yourself and how you may do things differently next time.

Getting Caught in Other People's Drama

Some people thrive in drama, while others retreat from it. If you find yourself in the middle of it, your best option is to remain neutral and say very little, if anything. After all, it is not your business. In the above Edible Arrangement example, I accepted that whatever dysfunction was occurring in their office existed long before I delivered the Edible Arrangement. Although the unfolding drama felt uncomfortable, I had not created it.

Apologize, Buy Another Gift, or Let It Go?

There is a time and a place to apologize. Saying sorry is appropriate when you have caused harm to another person, either verbally or physically, or you did not honor a commitment or meet an obligation after setting the expectation. This may pertain to over-promising on delivering a product or service for a client, making an error that was your responsibility, or making plans and subsequently not showing up, without explanation. In essence, you have let another person down through your own actions; therefore, it is incumbent upon you to take ownership.

If your best intentions go askew, blaming yourself for whatever transpires afterwards doesn't help you or your client. Nor is it helpful to say "should have, would have, could have." What is done is done. A more useful approach is to assess the situation and recognize what you learned about yourself and how you may do things differently next time.

However, if you intended to do the right thing and the end result was compromised in some fashion, due to events outside of your control, you have not wronged the other person. In the case of Allan, I thought long and hard about whether I should salvage the situation by buying another Edible Arrangement, or another gift that could be delivered without potentially causing him discomfort. I resolved matters in my own mind by coming to the realization that on that chilly day in December, my heart was in the right place. I had done my best and it was time to let go.

It's human nature to get caught up in a situation when you were the catalyst for the conflict. It is always important to remind yourself of your original intent, to make peace with yourself when everything goes awry, and to step away from the drama. Most importantly, as in every experience such as this, it's critical to look at the situation objectively and learn from your mistakes. Your experiences are your best teacher.

20

Room 142

Priorities Rule

"My legs are swollen and I don't feel like going up to the coffee shop today."

As soon as I heard my father utter those words on the telephone, thousands of miles away from his bed in the nursing home in Sydney, I knew that everything was different, even though I didn't want to believe what was happening. Dad was no longer able to dial my number, so I would call him instead, all too often finding him in his room. Time was slipping away.

My mother had endured a prolonged suffering in the same nursing home—ironically in the room right next door to Dad. She sadly had not lived to see her four beautiful grandchildren blossom into precious little people who would soon surround their grandfather by his bedside next door, succumbing to a similar fate, almost six years to the day later.

For weeks, I agonized over my decision to change my plans

and go home two months earlier than originally scheduled. I had endless conversations with the social workers, nurses, doctors, friends, my family—anyone who would listen in the hope they would convince me to stop procrastinating and just get on an airplane and fly home. I was in denial of the truth. Dad was dying and I couldn't bear it. It was easier to keep burying myself in my work and numb myself, rather than facing my unbearable sadness. Secretly, he knew by now that it was only a matter of time, and of course, I did as well.

We discovered that he had cancer when he was eighty-nine. My dad, who never endured any serious illnesses throughout his entire life, had survived the horrors of holocaust, and had lived through the most tumultuous economic hardships more than once, was not about to let this disease beat him when he first heard the diagnosis. In fact, he refused to believe it. He felt absolutely no symptoms whatsoever and his own doctor never suspected anything, even though the disease had no doubt been dormant for many years. Nonetheless, his doctor had some concerns regarding my father's mental state and in August 2009 made the decision to have him admitted to hospital for a thorough aged-care assessment.

Dad did not take kindly to undergoing a multitude of tests over the course of ten days, and bitterly complained that he wanted to go home. It was his persistent cough that caught the attention of medical staff. The diagnosis of bowel cancer as well as a secondary tumor in his lung left our family dumfounded. Dad refused to believe it because he didn't feel sick. Because of his feisty attitude, I, too, wondered if the test results were incorrect.

My brother, however, knew that there was no mistake. As he lived locally, he took it upon himself to organize my father's admission to the same nursing home where my mother had spent her last years. Because he was a palliative case, we were told that he would likely be admitted quickly. We were savvy enough to know that "quickly" meant between six months to a year.

How do you tell your fiercely independent parent this news? How do you help him accept it? What do you do to prepare him for the inevitable reality that the next place is the final place? As a grown woman who now had to "parent" her own parent, how was I to compartmentalize the actuality of the situation into my busy life, while allowing the excruciating grief of impending loss to rise to the surface? I had to accept reality. I knew that soon, I was to face being an adult orphan.

I had last visited my father in August 2010. He was by then a resident of the nursing home and although he was a palliative case, there was no need for him to be placed in critical care, at least not initially. My husband accompanied me on that trip and we were both relieved and delighted to see that he had put on weight and was receiving excellent care.

Dad adapted to the rituals and surroundings and the staff adored him. He charmed them with his life stories and sense of humor. They admired the fact that every day he was decked out in one of his business suits (and the occasional tie) to have lunch in the elegantly set dining room. Dad's attire was fitting for the occasion as he sat at the table, adorned with white-linen tableclothes and flowers. Classical music played in the background. The staff felt it was their duty to ensure that every meal was a dignified, special experience.

One of Dad's closest friends, Herman Fischer, was also in the same section of the nursing home. Herman had run a highly successful business as a tailor. His handmade, high-end suits were the only ones my father would wear. Dad's business partner, Tony Dale, was in the section upstairs for those requiring a higher level of care. Tony had helped my father forty years earlier by taking him in as a partner in his retail clothing stores when dad was unemployed.

I never could have imagined that all three men would be spending their final years in the same nursing home. Yet there they were: strong and vital members of their generation, together in what would become the place they ultimately would bid each other goodbye. The unexpected and remarkable reunion of this triumvirate seemed unreal to me. I am certain they never dreamed of this outcome, nor could our respective families. However, we came to appreciate that they were together, despite the circumstances.

There was no question that Dad was the best-dressed man, surrounded by a bevvy of elderly ladies, one of whom became his constant companion for regular rounds of gin rummy and concerts in the main hall. After my mother passed away, Dad had endured years of loneliness. Although I was heartbroken upon hearing the cancer verdict, I was comforted knowing that he had company and friendship until the end.

Priorities Rule

Finally, I made up my mind to spend time with my father while he was still conscious. Had I not done so, I knew that it would have been one of my greatest regrets. This was my highest priority and nothing was going to stop me from getting on the plane. Earlier on the day of my departure, I had conducted a three-hour training session. I told the meeting planner as well as the entire audience what I was about to do. I wanted them to know that priorities rule. I did not care about paying the change fee on my airline ticket that was originally booked for a later date.

When I boarded the plane for Australia, I could barely wait to get there. I arrived in Sydney after the long flight and immediately headed to the nursing home. I walked into the dining room just at the end of the lunch hour.

The sight of my father walking toward me, with every ounce of energy he could muster, supported by his walker, took my breath away. The drastic change in his countenance since I'd last seen him just six months earlier was astonishing. I fought back the tears as I looked at his withering form, and hugged him close. He was wearing a navy blue suit, the one he had worn on my wedding day four years prior. Only this time, it was hanging from his body.

I stayed by his bedside for five consecutive days. He slept a great deal and told me he knew he was going to die. His feet were severely swollen and it was extremely difficult for him to stand up, let alone walk. Morphine was introduced for the first time. My father was experiencing tremendous pain as the cancer was advancing rapidly. The doctor explained that the cancerous mass engulfing his lungs was now quickly spreading. The X-rays brought home the horrific reality. His long-standing cough had now become a gurgling sound, drowning out any attempt Dad would make to communicate.

My brother also visited him daily, along with his wife and four children. We reflected on Dad's life, laughing out loud as we recalled his passion for chicken schnitzel and the fact that he expected every restaurant (and bar) to have it on the menu. I told them stories about Dad's many visits to Canada and how my husband and I went to great lengths to ensure that his quirky meal requests would be satisfied. The life he'd lived—one that was joyous, turbulent, sorrowful, enchanting, exhilarating, and often laborious—was now culminating in this tiny room, surrounded by those closest to him. It was an honor and privilege I wouldn't have missed for the world.

Doing the Right Things versus Doing Things Right

How many of us can honestly say that we are living life with no regrets? Do we appreciate every moment we experience with those closest to us? Are we able to cherish the memories and fondly reflect on the milestones? Are we comfortable with our own decisions, as opposed to second-guessing ourselves, rehashing what could have been . . . *if only*? Have we made peace with our past?

I recall the significance of sharing the turn of the millennium with my mother and dad in Australia. I felt safe and comforted in my mother's kitchen, and surrounded by the pure joy she experienced preparing my favorite dishes, I marveled at the fact that my parents had lived to see the dawning of a new century. Later that night, we watched the famous fireworks over the Sydney Harbour Bridge live on TV and toasted the New Year together. There was great fanfare on the screen, but sitting there in the living room, sharing the simplicity of the evening after a meal of mother's home cooking, surpassed any fanfare or celebration I could imagine. Home sweet home.

When we are very clear about the most important things and take the appropriate actions, we have no remorse. We are leading ourselves and our conscience is clear. Being at peace is the priceless gift we can give ourselves whenever we choose.

Guilt—A Wasted Expenditure of Energy

Living a guilt-free life is a lofty goal. I have yet to encounter anyone who has not felt guilty at some point, myself included. Unfortunately, many people are unable to let go of this emotion because they lack confidence in themselves and their ability to make a decision and stick with it. We are constantly being pulled in a myriad of directions as we try to find balance.

For example, I can say unequivocally that when I am taking

care of my grandchildren, I enjoy them immensely and hang onto every fun moment we share. However, my primary relationship is with my husband. As we both precariously juggle a busy work schedule with time for ourselves as well as personal commitments, there are times when saying "no" to babysitting and "yes" to time for the two of us is fundamentally important.

When I experience the emotional "pull" to help out, I am mindful that my decision has consequences. If I am exhausted or find myself going to great lengths to accommodate, then I risk experiencing an unwelcome but familiar emotion to each of us: resentment. The two go hand-in-hand. The solution lies in knowing the highest priorities in that moment, ensuring that I pay heed to them by taking charge of myself, and as a result, make guilt-free choices. Should I make the "wrong" choice, berating myself serves no purpose whatsoever.

> *When we are very clear about the most important things and take the appropriate actions, we have no remorse. We are leading ourselves and our conscience is clear. Being at peace is the priceless gift we can give ourselves whenever we choose.*

Moments of Truth

Being at the crossroads when assessing personal or professional priorities and subsequently taking action on them is an opportunity to look in the mirror. Practicing personal leadership necessitates self-reflection. These moments are moments of truth. They may come in the form of a pivotal, life-altering moment that is occurring for reasons that may not be immediately clear. At some point, the reason may be revealed, or perhaps, it may remain a mystery.

Being present for the passing of our parents is not something we think about frequently during childhood and much of our adult lives. When I realized the moment of death was close at hand for both my mother and dad, it was an overwhelming and painful experience. However, I understood that I was exactly where I was meant to me. The fact that they knew I was in the room was a comfort to them. There could be no greater moment of truth.

21

Leading Yourself Means *Being Yourself*

Today you are You, that's truer than true.
There is no one alive who is Youer than You.

—DR. SEUSS

It was a beautiful (albeit typically rainy) month of June in Vancouver. The dismal weather didn't bother me that year, however, for it soon was to be my wedding day. As the rain poured outside, I was excited to hear the sounds of children playing in my apartment. My father, my brother, and his wife had traveled from Australia for the occasion with their children, all under the age of six (who incidentally never recovered from the jetlag during their entire two-week stay at my place!). I had moved out in order to give them the space they needed to make themselves at home. DVDs were sprawled across the carpet in my living room, along with an assortment of clothes, toys, diapers, candy wrappers, and leftovers.

Total chaos reigned and I could hardly wait to be a part of

the fun as I arrived at my own doorstep for our daily visits. One morning, my six-year-old niece came running as she heard me knocking at the door. I was greeted with a huge hug and couldn't help but notice she was wearing her five-year-old brother's Spider-man cape and her mother's high-heeled shoes that were part of her "wedding outfit." She and her siblings had been awake for hours, ready to take on the day, playing together and delighting in delving into the wardrobe and amusing themselves. They did not need any adult's approval as they made their own unique fashion statements. I marveled at the fact that they were totally comfortable being themselves.

What happens to our ability to exude this type of confidence that we innately possess in early childhood and begin to lose once we start elementary school? Why do we begin to pay attention to what others think, yearning for consent and approval? At what point do many of us become so concerned about achieving the acceptance and permission to be ourselves from a society that is conditioned to pass judgement on our appearance or the sound of our voice in a matter of seconds?

The impact of losing that childlike celebration of our quintessential spirit can be devastating. It happens on a daily basis, often without our conscious awareness. As others begin to reject us, we begin to reject ourselves. We often become preoccupied with approval-seeking without realizing the consequences to our self-esteem and ultimately, our career path. In effect, we forget how to lead ourselves first.

Earlier in this book, I described various scenarios of my parents emigrating to a new country, beginning a new life after the devastation of war, loss, and humiliating experiences that shook them both to their core. The remnants of shame and degradation they carried in the aftermath were often compounded in everyday business and life situations. I recall my mother telling me stories about customers who would come into her store and upon hearing her "foreign" accent, would speak slowly or awkwardly, mimicking her twang, as if she were incapable of speaking the same language. She would be deeply embarrassed by these encounters, although ironically she spoke better English than many of her patrons due to her level of education, passion for cryptic crosswords, and love of reading.

> *As others begin to reject us, we begin to reject ourselves. We often become preoccupied with approval-seeking without realizing the consequences to our self-esteem and ultimately, our career path. In effect, we forget how to lead ourselves first.*

My mother's experience was certainly not unique. I recently worked with a client who invited me to speak to an audience they described as visible minorities. Their organization is recognized as an industry leader in the area of celebrating and promoting diversity. My client provided me with a brief for their annual event with the objective of encouraging their team of managers to eradicate self-doubt and build self-confidence in order to be the best leaders possible. It was important to recognize developing a mindset of inclusiveness; to appreciate differences and deliver a message with universal appeal. We decided on a presentation title: *Leadership Begins with Me*. This became the event theme and the afternoon was a great success.

I admired my client's philosophy and ability to truly "walk the talk" regarding creating and maintaining an all-embracing culture. As part of the event wrap-up, the chair invited a senior member of their leadership team on stage for an informal Q & A. He spoke candidly about his career and personal background as an immigrant. Surprisingly, when asked about his level of awareness as part of a visible minority group, the leader admitted to the audience that there are still occasions in a business setting where he feels some level of discomfort regarding his ethnicity. His example stood out for me, as I recalled my mother's feelings of shame about her accent. I silently wondered whether his message and heartfelt admission regarding questioning his own authenticity had a similar impact on others in the audience?

Promoting, respecting, and honoring differences—whether they pertain to culture, gender, or sexual orientation—is now thankfully commonplace in many organizations. Encouraging authenticity, however, presents a different set of challenges due to the fact that workplaces establish a particular culture with the objective of developing teams whose values mesh well with those of their employer. Teams, of course, are comprised of individuals who posses their own beliefs and attitudes that may not always conform to the norm. Therefore, the pressure to play the game doesn't go away when individual needs are sacrificed for the group.

One's unique identity cannot be completely suppressed unless we, as individuals, make that choice. Whether it is a matter of culture, or simply having a different point of view on any particular subject, the need for creative self-expression is innate.

The potential for conflict escalation, low morale in the workplace, and a demoralized self-esteem are the consequences of choosing not to *lead ourselves* and *be ourselves*. Conversely, the impact of letting our true selves shine in every arena of our lives is a far more desirable alternative. It begins by practicing self-acceptance, capturing the essence of our response to the world as children and cherishing the magical perspective that is our birthright, unaffected by the opinions of others and energized by the world around us as if nothing else mattered.

Early on in this book, I introduced you to Stan the Man as an illustration of someone who, as I wrote, personified the meaning of "leader" as he harnessed the ability to take charge of his thoughts, and consequently his actions, in any situation. I also mentioned that after his initial e-mail to me subsequent to a seemingly inconsequential meeting in that airport security line, we carried on a long and rich correspondence that I will treasure as long as I live.

Stan was one of those rare individuals who leave a lasting "heartprint" on our souls forever. Once again, in his words, he wished to "continue to make a difference" in the lives of others.

In closing, and in honor of Stan's wish, I'd like to share with you his final e-mail message to me. May it serve as a reminder that we each have been given the gift of life. And the greatest gift is the one we give to ourselves when we choose to lead ourselves first.

-----*Original Message*-----
From: Stan Lindley
Sent: Monday, November 19, 2007 11:40 PM
To: Michelle Ray
Subject: Re: From Michelle Ray speaker in Vancouver

Well, hi there!

First of all let me congratulate you on your marriage. That's great! I hope you are so happy. I know in my heart you deserve it. Well, I am still on this side of the grass. As I'm sure you remember I am dealing with a severe form of Cancer. Since Remberance Day it's been exactly one year since I found out. Been quite a year. Lots of operations that didn't work, and then Chemo which didn't do a thing, and now I'm on a kind of an experimental thing which just might keep me around for another month or so. Two months ago after failed Chemo my son Keith, and my ex wife were with me to hear I may have only 3–4 months left. Now with the new stuff who knows . . .

I want to live Michelle, I want to love again, I want to see my Grand Daughters grow up . . . and I am going to do what I have to do. . . . The big push is alternative treatments and on and on it goes . . . but I'm staying to course, no corrections, and faith in my God and the Doctors. For some reason that seems to bug some folks. . . . But I'm an old fart and I have watched friends die trying all these weird and strange things . . .

I was so good at my job at the Airport, even though it was demeaning to me . . . because of my past, but I endured just to try and make a difference. Sadly when I got the 3–4 month thing I had to quit. The job has spiraled through the stair case though. It's so sad what is happening. Morale does not exist. A female friend of mine was going through Victoria not long ago and somehow ticked off the Guards. She has a bad heart and a pacemaker. They forced her to go through the Walk Through Metal Detector which is a huge no-no and could have really messed her up (or killed her!!!). They should have all been fired . . . but that's what it has become. It's all window dressing Michelle, and now it's totally non-professional.

I know . . . I should be talking with my MP but it's useless. The Government appears to be in on it. And who am I . . .

a disgruntled forced out former employee . . . they would make me look like an idiot.

O.k. Stan get back in the box!! . . . so there you go my friend, just know that the horror stories you have heard about airport security are true . . . and on that note I will say TTFN, *and I really do hope I hear from you again. You are a very neat person and I am especially glad to have met you. . . . It means a lot to me that you are satisfied and happy. I just hope it is so. I am well and a bit crusty . . . but what the heck . . . . . . with my background I know too much.*

God Bless you,
Your Prairie Dog Buddy,
Stan

References

Chapter 2

Keown, Leslie-Anne, "Time escapes me: Workaholics and time perception," Statistics Canada, http://www.statcan.gc.ca/pub/11-008-x/2007001/9629-eng.htm

Snopek, David, "American Stereotypes: Americans are Workaholics," Blog, http://www.linguatrek.com/blog/2011/09/american-stereotypes-americans-are-workaholics

Chapter 4

"The New Employment Deal: How Far, How Fast and How Enduring: Insights from Towers Watson's 2010 Global Workforce Study," TowersWatson.com, http://www.towerswatson.com/global-workforce-study/

"15 Home Business Ideas that Thrive During Recession," Powerhomebiz.com, http://www.powerhomebiz.com/News/062009/home-business-ideas-recession.htm

"Top 25 Careers to Pursue in a Recession," HRworld.com, http://www.hrworld.com/features/top-25-recession-careers-022008/

Chapter 7

Santayana, George. *The Life of Reason*. Toronto: University of Toronto Libraries. 2011.

"Ninja Generation." Blog post January 24, 2011. Ninjageneration.com http://ninjageneration.com/2011/01/ninja-generation/

Chapter 8

"Walt Disney Biography," JustDisney.com, http://www.justdisney.com/walt_disney/biography/long_bio.html

"Walt Disney," Wikipedia.com, http://en.wikipedia.org/wiki/Walt_Disney

Chapter 9

Almasy, Steve. "Days after mother's death, Olympic figure skater pushes on." CNN.com, http://www.cnn.com/2010/SPORT/02/24/olympics.rochette/index.html

Jayson, Sharon, "Americans are resilient, even after tragedies as big as 9/11," *USA Today*, Usaedition, http://www.usatoday.com/LIFE/usaedition/2011-08-04-APA-cover--Emotional-effects-of-9-11_CV_U.htm

Michael Jordan Quotes, BrainyQuote.com http://www.brainyquote.com/quotes/quotes/m/michaeljor127660.html#HqhoOzloUIbtdL6A.99

Chapter 10

"The Rosenberg Self-Esteem Scale," University of Maryland, Department of Sociology, http://www.bsos.umd.edu/socy/research/rosenberg.htm

Bandura, A. *Self-Efficacy in Changing Societies.* Cambridge University Press. 1995.

Chapter 13

"Military Leaders on Leadership," Safetyrisk.com, http://www.safetyrisk.com.au/2012/02/06/military-leaders-on-leadership/

Chapter 16:

Neill, James. "What Is Locus of Control?" Wilderdom.com http://wilderdom.com/psychology/loc/LocusOfControlWhatIs.html

"Amygdala," Wikipedia.org, http://en.wikipedia.org/wiki/Amygdala

Decker, Bert. *You've Got to Be Believed to Be Heard*. St. Martins Press. 2008.

Phelps, Jim, M.D., "Fear" PsychEductation.org, http://www.psycheducation.org/emotion/amygdala.htm

Chapter 18

"The Latest Job Satisfaction Stats," Escape from Corporate America blog, http://www.escapefromcorporate.com/the-latest-job-satisfaction-stats/

Pepitone, Julianne. "U.S. job satisfaction hits 22-year low," CNNmoney.com, http://money.cnn.com/2010/01/05/news/economy/job_satisfaction_report/

Lee, Thomas W., Mitchell, Terence R., Holtom, Brooks C., Inderrieden, Edward J. "Shocks as Causes of Turnover: What They Are and How Organizations Can Manage Them," *Human Resources Management*, Fall 2005, Vol. 44, No. 3, pp. 337–338.

About the Author

Born in Australia, Michelle Ray is the Founder and CEO of the *Lead Yourself First Institute*. Michelle is a leadership and workplace relationship expert who demonstrates a deep understanding of personal accountability, internal team dynamics, interpersonal communication, and service excellence. She uses an interactive approach to inspire and captivate the imagination of her audiences.

Michelle began her career in the media industry during the recession of the early 1980s. She was once told by management that she "didn't have what it takes" to succeed in the business world. Despite a lack of mentors, Michelle was inspired to move up the management ladder to self-employment, eventually creating her own successful international business.

Michelle's first training, speaking and consulting company was established in 1995. She subsequently created the *Lead Yourself First Institute* to help individuals and organizations take the initiative in the face of change and economic uncertainty. Her company's array of educational training and keynote topics specialize in areas she describes as high demand essentials for professional growth. Michelle also offers in-house business seminars and consulting for leadership development, understanding changing demographics, communication and improving workplace relationships.

Michelle is a Certified Speaking Professional (CSP), the highest-earned designation in the speaking industry. Less than 600 people worldwide have earned this distinction after meeting rigorous criteria established by the National Speakers' Association. She has been listed in the Who's Who of Professional Speakers and has worked with a myriad of clientele providing in house seminars and conference presentations. Her style has been described as refreshing, uplifting, entertaining, informative and amusing with a common sense message.

From thousands of entries received, Michelle reached the "Top Ten" of North America's Next Greatest Speaker Contest in 2012. She currently resides in Vancouver, British Columbia with her husband Brian, is an avid runner, and enjoys spending time with her two adorable grandchildren.

Tell Me Your Story

A personal message from Michelle

Now that you've read my book, I would love to hear your personal story.

I hope my message has impacted your life in a positive way, both personally and professionally. What changes have you made in your communication, business relationships or career? If you have been inspired to start a new business, how did my book help create the impetus needed to transform your thinking and motivate you to take action?

Your words of inspiration will inspire others to realize their potential and fulfill their dreams. Please email your success story to michelle@leadyourselfist.com for the opportunity to be nominated into the *Lead Yourself First Institute Hall of Fame*.

I look forward to hearing from you!

Michelle